THE MAGIC OF LONDON'S MUSEUMS

by John Lucas

Exley Publications

By the same author:
Backs to the Garden Wall (Stanley Paul,
Hutchinson, 1966)
The Big Umbrella (Elm Tree Books,
Hamish Hamilton, 1973)

*To Christopher and Jonathan, in the
hope that they — and all teachers,
parents and children everywhere — will
always make time to stand and stare.*

Contents

PHOTOGRAPHS
Cover photograph of Triceratops, at the Natural History Museum, by Richard Exley.

Our thanks go to all the museums in the book who have generously given us permission to use the photographs which appear with their entries. Copyright in all cases is reserved.

We also thank the following for the use of their photographs:

British Tourist Authority: pages 18, 21, 99, 117, 141

Charles Skilton & Fry Ltd: page 155

Crown copyright: pages 11, 16, 27, 58, 78, 114, 119, 120, 121, 144, 145, 148, 149, 150, 154

Norman Derrick: page 105

English Life Publications Ltd: page 57

Richard Exley: page 112

John Lucas: pages 12, 13, 59, 81

National Portrait Gallery: pages 10, 46

Thorpe Model Makers Ltd: pages 89, 91 (top)

The Warburg Institute: page 70

Notes about practical details

There is a wide variation in provisions for bank holiday opening, and for space reasons individual details have not been given. A telephone check with museums is advisable if there is any doubt.

Inflation has made it impossible to state the price of admission with any certainty where this applies; in fact, most places are free to visit. I have therefore simply stated 'admission charge' or 'free admission'.

Bus routes may not cover every day of the week or every part of the day. A check can be made on a London Transport bus map or on time-tables at bus stops.

Author's Introduction

To tour nearly a hundred museums, galleries and historic houses, as I have done, is an unforgettable experience. I recall the array of precious stones in the Geological Museum; the violins that play themselves mechanically in the National Musical Museum; the glory of Robert Adam's work at Osterley Park House and Kenwood; the Apollo 10 moon-shot capsule in the Science Museum; and the galleries, fertile with beauty at every turn, in the Victoria & Albert Museum.

Such pleasures are available to all, and at small, if any, cost. Of these places, little more than a third make any charge at all: then usually only the minimum required for adequate servicing and maintenance.

At one time the word 'museum' had overtones of dust and dullness. If it has today, it is undeserved. In recent years strenuous efforts have been made by museums and galleries to refurbish themselves and mount bigger, more ambitiously designed, more informative and more entertaining exhibitions than ever before for their young and inquisitive public.

Many of the museums also have educational departments, which help to feed children's curiosity with talks, films — and even Saturday morning clubs.

The descriptions that follow are not intended to be comprehensive, nor to render redundant the museums' own informative handbooks. What I have tried to provide is a handy signpost to what interesting or important (or sometimes both) exhibits there are to be seen and where — in places you might never have thought existed. If as a result of thumbing through these pages you are stirred to make your own voyages of discovery in London, then I shall consider my own marathon trek, already thoroughly rewarding, to have yielded a bonus.

John Lucas

A Victorian photographer (Kodak Museum).

Back to Saxon times and beyond

Relics of Roman London and the Plague under the City's most ancient tower

This old church, much damaged during World War II, is the headquarters church of Toc H and stands within the shadow of the Tower of London. Its Saxon origins are evident on the way to the Undercroft, which contains the church's historical collection.

To the left is a splendid Saxon arch of Roman bonding tiles (the builders knew nothing of keystones), which formed part of the church's original tower — the oldest in the City — dated *c* AD 675.

The Undercroft contains portions of two tessellated Roman floors and evidence of the foundations of the Saxon tower. There is a Roman tombstone, with the inscription: *To Demetrius: Heracula his wife set up this stone at the expense of her own estate.*

There is an excellent diorama of Roman London, together with many artifacts: a Roman coin bearing Nero's head, the cornice of a pillar found near the Forum (where Leadenhall Market now stands), roofing tiles, cooking vessels, Roman lamps, styli pens, Samian-ware dishes and bowls and the make-up implements of a Roman lady.

Two famous names appear in the church registers on display: William Penn, founder of Pennsylvania, is named in the Baptismal Register for the 23rd October 1644. Penn's father, an admiral, 22 years later helped to quench the flames of the Great Fire as it licked the west wall of All Hallows, thus saving the church from destruction. The other name is that of John Quincy Adams, sixth president of the United States of America, who was married here on the 27th July 1797 to Louisa Catherine Johnson.

Two contemporary records appear in the original. The church's second register is open at September 1665, the year of the dreaded Great Plague, showing 94 names of those who had died that month within the parish boundary. An extract from the churchwardens' accounts between 1628 and 1666 throws an interesting light upon inflation. 'Five stone of Beef, three legs of Mutton, two quarters of Lamb and three capons and paid Mr Davis for dressing Dinner and for Wine' — all for £4 9s 10d! Also on show is a silver trowel used by Queen Elizabeth II when laying the foundation stone of the rebuilt church.

Practical details: Undercroft is open on Saturday and Sunday between 10.30 am and 5.30 pm, except during services. Weekday opening hours are 9.30 am to 5.30 pm whenever a guide is available. (Visitors *must* be accompanied by a guide.) Large parties by appointment only, when there is a small charge per head. Nearest British Rail station is Fenchurch Street (ER), and nearest Underground station is Tower Hill. Use buses 42 or 78.

Address: Byward Street EC3R 5BJ. Telephone (01) 481 2928:

BADEN-POWELL HOUSE

The founder of Scouting

Memories of Baden-Powell, leader of soldiers and young people

Those of us who are over 40 and were members of the Scout movement in youth will remember with sadness 8th January 1941, the day the founder, 'B-P' (Lord Baden-Powell) died. But of course B-P has lived on in many ways. The Scouts are his abiding memorial. Another, more recent, is Baden-Powell House, marked out from other buildings in Queen's Gate by a fine statue of a hatless B-P, sculpted in granite by Don Potter. Baden-Powell House's principal function is that of a hostel for Scouts visiting London. It also houses a permanent exhibition of relics — a fascinating chronicle of the founder and the movement from the earliest days.

The exhibition begins, logically, with displays concerning B-P's childhood — a sketch of his birthplace in London, his birth certificate, and a book, *Stories About Animals*, which he wrote and illustrated at the age of nine.

As a young man, Baden-Powell was commissioned into the 13th Hussars and served in the Mediterranean and Africa. Mementoes of his stay there include photographs and sketches (he was a competent artist as well as writer), and relics of Mafeking, relieved when B-P was in command of the besieged force. On display are ration tickets, some chocolate sent out by Queen Victoria, a bugle, shell and cartridges as used in the town's defence, together with B-P's Hussar uniform.

For Baden-Powell, scouting really began in 1897 with methods introduced to train NCOs and men to be self-reliant. He was able to put these into practice during the siege, and even more after the famous experimental Brownsea Island camp of 1907. This is marked in the exhibition by a diorama, photographs and the rallying Kudu horn brought back from Matabeleland by B-P. Scouting was soon a firmly established feature of national life. B-P's first hat badge and shoulder knots are on show, and the manuscript of *Scouting for Boys,* the movement's 'Bible', along with an early issue of *The Scout* magazine, and cuttings and drawings connected with B-P's knighthood.

Many exhibits demonstrate the work of Scouts in the two world wars, including Jack Cornwell's Scout VC (see also Imperial War Museum, page 66).

At the Coming-of-Age Jamboree held at Arrowe Park, Birkenhead, in 1929, Scouts from all over the world subscribed to buy the Chief a car — a Rolls Royce — and caravan. A scale model of the car (named 'Jam Roll' by B-P) is on show, and a letter from the Chief to Princess Elizabeth. Finally, there are B-P's last recorded message in three languages and a display of photographs of his funeral and burial on the slopes of the Aberdares facing Mount Kenya.

Practical details: Open daily, by appointment, from 9 am to 6 pm. Free admission. Nearby Underground stations are Gloucester Road and South Kensington. Use buses 14, 30, 52, 73 or 74. Refreshments available.

Address: Queen's Gate, South Kensington SW7 5JS. Telephone (01) 584 7030.

Lord Baden-Powell, the founder of the Scout movement.

BANQUETING HOUSE

Last moments of a king

Rubens' triumphant tribute to king and government

Detail from the glorious Rubens ceiling at the Banqueting House.

It was on a scaffold erected in front of the present entrance to the Banqueting House in Whitehall that Charles I was executed in 1649. Minutes before, Charles had suffered the unhappy irony of walking beneath the glorious ceiling paintings by Rubens — the very ones he had commissioned 20 years before and which are heavily symbolic of the benefits of wise Stuart monarchy. They show the Benefits of James I's Government and his Apotheosis, which are best seen from the north end of the hall; and the Union of England and Scotland, best seen from the south. The oval pictures in the angles show: Royal Bounty bestriding Avarice; Wise Government curbing Intemperate Discord; Heroic Virtue clubbing Rebellion, and Heroic Wisdom impaling Ignorance. Two panels showing the procession of cherubs, representing Joyous Prosperity, are best seen from opposite sides of the hall.

The Banqueting House, a triumph of architecture by Inigo Jones completed in 1622, has recently undergone restoration, and is once more an assembly place for great occasions, a purpose close to its original one of presence chamber of the Stuarts. Performances of masques (with stage settings by Inigo Jones) were originally given here. With the appearance of Rubens' ceiling paintings, the masques were transferred to an adjacent building in case the paintings were damaged by smoke from the stage lamps.

The Banqueting House once formed part of the Palace of Whitehall, which was the London home of reigning monarchs between 1530 and 1698, when it became a Chapel Royal.

Practical details: Open from Tuesday to Saturday, 10 am to 5 pm, and on Sunday from 2 to 5 pm. There is an admission charge. Nearest British Rail station is Charing Cross (SR). Nearby Underground stations are Embankment, Trafalgar Square and Westminster. Use buses 3, 11, 12, 24, 29, 53, 76, 77, 88 or 168.

Address: Whitehall SW1A 2ER.

BARNET MUSEUM

Where Warwick fought

Reminders of the Wars of the Roses among household goods of different periods

In 1471 the Earl of Warwick was killed when his army was defeated in the Battle of Barnet, one of the last of the Wars of the Roses. An obelisk marks the site on Hadley Common, a verdant spot just outside the town.

Barnet Museum is in the town itself, and relics of the battle can be seen. There are a cannonball and some musketoon shot, found 8 feet below the surface at Hadley, but these are of uncertain date; and there is a medieval helmet, found in 1879, though Tower of London armoury experts set it at some years after the battle. A series of replicas of banners carried by the Earl and his opponent, Edward IV, are displayed: these were made for the 500th anniversary celebrations of the battle in 1971.

This museum offers surprises at every turn. A small room furnished throughout in heavy Victorian style; a clutch of corn dollies, a group of photographs and drawings of a German airship being brought down at Potters Bar in 1916, together with sections of the metal skeleton. There is a fine collection of horseshoes from the Middle Ages onwards, given by a local veterinary surgeon, and a 'human' shoe, dating from the fourteenth century, found five feet down in the High Street.

Old implements and instruments, household and otherwise, are on show, including sewing machines. There are collections of nineteenth-century women's dresses and Brazilian butterflies, an Almanack of 1672, Coronation mugs and plates, and some Maundy money. Near the museum stands Tudor Hall, a sixteenth-century building: part of an early roof, locks and keys are preserved in the museum, along with panelling and part of the Minstrels' Gallery.

Practical details: Open on Tuesday and Thursday between 2.30 and 4.30 pm, also on Saturday from 10 am to 12.30 pm and from 2.30 to 4.30 pm. Free admission. Nearest Underground station is High Barnet. Use buses 34, 84, 107, 134 or 263.

Address: Wood Street, Barnet EN5 4BE.

Where Warwick the Kingmaker was slain.

12

BEAR GARDENS MUSEUM AND ARTS CENTRE

Elizabethan Theatreland

This museum, near the site of the old Globe, is devoted to the theatre of Shakespeare, Jonson and their contemporaries

Less than 100 yards from the site of Shakespeare's Globe theatre is a small but interesting museum dedicated to the development and influence of the English theatre up to the mid-seventeenth century. Opened in 1972 and extended in 1977-78, the Bear Gardens Museum is itself on the site of a Jacobean playhouse, a rival of the Globe called the Hope. Earlier, the last bear-baiting ring on Bankside stood here.

The first Globe is displayed modelled in the familiar polygonal shape with apron stage and a thatched roof. It was burnt down in 1613 during a performance of *Henry VIII,* and a sonnet written the next day ran:

> *Be warned you stage strutters all,*
> *Least you again be catched,*
> *And such a burning doe befall*
> *As to them whose house was*
> *thatched.*

So a second Globe, shown in the Museum in its tiled-roof form, was built 'far fairer than before', the next year. Apparently there were other dangers in playgoing than fire, for a proclamation by Queen Elizabeth I — an original printed poster of July 1580 can be seen — warned of the danger of catching the Plague when visiting the common playhouse.

The models are skilfully fashioned:

How the first Globe theatre might have looked.

there is one of the Swan and Fortune playhouses which, with the Globe, were all within 100 yards of each other. There is also a beautiful atmospheric scene of the Thames Frost Fair, complete with stalls on the frozen river, and timbered houses — and the theatres — clustered on the South Bank.

Visitors will find plenty of information here on Shakespeare and his contemporaries in the contexts of theatrical, political and court circles of the late sixteenth and seventeenth centuries. A display, which includes a history of the original Cockpit Playhouse, is being reconstructed in full-size model form.

Following on from Shakespeare and his friendship with Jonson is a section on architect Inigo Jones, and the Court Masques (many of which Jones designed) before the theatres were closed down by Oliver Cromwell in 1642.

There are several interesting reproductions of old map engravings, together with a modern photograph of the South Bank from the air, pinpointing the positions of the old playhouses. Contributing to the Shakespearean flavour of the museum is a facsimile copy of the first folio of his plays, dated 1623.

Practical details: Open Monday to Friday from 10.30 am to 5.30 pm, and on Saturday and Sunday from 11 am to 5 pm. There is an admission charge. Nearby British Rail *and* Underground stations are Cannon Street (SR), Waterloo (SR) and London Bridge (SR). Use buses 10, 18, 35, 40, 44, 47, 48, 70, 95, 133, 149 or 176A.

Address: 1 Bear Gardens, Bankside, Southwark SE1 9ED. Telephone (01) 928 6342.

HMS BELFAST

World War II cruiser

The last surviving World War II warship shows herself off . . . from Admiral's bridge to engine room

In 1971 the 11,550-ton cruiser *Belfast* won her last battle, when she was saved from the scrapyard by the combined forces of the Imperial War Museum and public opinion. Now this historic ship, the last surviving warship of the last war, is moored in the Thames, almost opposite the Tower of London.

Belfast saw plenty of action in her time. She was launched by Mrs Neville Chamberlain, wife of the then Prime Minister, in March 1939, and less than three months after war began was badly damaged by a magnetic mine. After rebuilding, she became an escort ship for convoys to Russia, and fired the first rounds in the Battle of North Cape, in which the German battleship *Scharnhorst* was sunk. In June 1944 her guns helped to cover the Normandy landings. Later, she served in the Korean War.

HMS Belfast, the cruiser that helped to sink the Scharnhorst.

The best way for visitors to see the *Belfast* is to follow the sign-posted route round her. The ship has been preserved as far as possible as she was. The port torpedo tubes, from which three hits were scored on *Scharnhorst,* have disappeared, but her twelve six-inch guns, in four triple mountings, are all there. The four turrets can be inspected, and continuous tape-recordings simulate the use of the guns in action. The shells for these, raised automatically from magazines below, weighed one hundredweight each.

The six-inch guns were the cruiser's primary armament. For use against air attack, or for short-range combat, there were twelve four-inch guns, eight of which remain.

The tour begins with the fo'c'sle, where visitors can see the huge anchor and cables and then climb up to the gun turrets. The guns were controlled and fired from the gun direction platform, with its many instruments for communication and taking bearings on targets.

The bridge and compass platform formed the nerve centre of the ship. Here the Captain presided. Below him, because *Belfast* was a flagship, was the bridge of the flag officer (usually an Admiral), from which he directed the activities of the fleet. One can visit the operations room, which fed the Captain with information; the bridge wireless office, and the forward steering position which contains the ship's wheel. In the ship's museum *Belfast's* history, and that of cruisers generally, is described in photograph and chart. *Belfast* took part in the invasion of Europe (Operation Overlord, p 115),

and a special exhibition tells of
the preparations for D-Day in June
1944. Special exhibitions feature
mines and a 21-inch torpedo of the
type with which *Belfast* was armed,
24-feet long.
Visitors can also see the mess-decks,
where the ratings once ate, lived and
slept. Two 'mock-ups' of messes show
the inferior conditions of 1939 and the
1950s compared with the more
comfortable quarters of today. The
sick bay, dental surgery and galley,
where meals were prepared, can also
be seen.
In the bowels of the ship are the boiler
and engine rooms, which have been
restored and give some indication of
their enormous capacity and power
when under steam. They can drive the
ship to a maximum speed of 32 knots.
Near the end of the tour is the Chapel
(provided for every ship of cruiser size
and above), which always remained
open. Look out for the upturned bell,
serving as a font. The *Belfast's* own
silver bell, now on display, was
recently returned by the people of
Belfast, where the ship was built in
1938.
A new permanent exhibition,
'Conflict at Sea', of 60 paintings by
John Hamilton, was due to open
aboard *Belfast* in the spring of 1979.
Practical details: In summer, open
daily from 11 am to 5.50 pm, and in
winter daily from 11 am to 4.30 pm.
There is an admission charge. Nearest
British Rail station is London Bridge
(SR). Nearby Underground stations
are London Bridge, Monument and
Tower Hill. Use buses 10, 42, 46, 48, 70
or 78. Refreshments available.
Address: Symons Wharf, Vine Lane
SE1 2JH. Telephone (01) 407 6434 or
(01) 735 8922.

BETHNAL GREEN MUSEUM OF CHILDHOOD

Memories of youth

Children's clothes, dolls, toys and bridal dresses through the ages

The unprepossessing area in which
the museum stands is no indication of
the many delights in store for the
grown-up or young visitor to this
branch of the Victoria & Albert
Museum (see page 147).
Children's interest will be quickly

*The museum has the most
comprehensive collection of dolls in
Britain.*

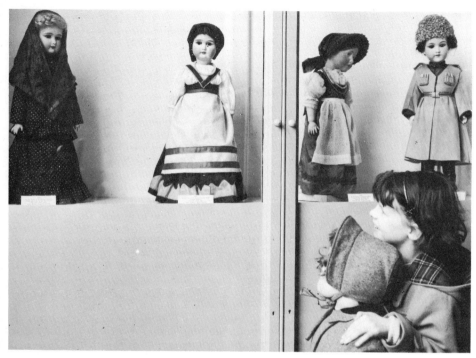

There are two centuries of children's costumes, from the 1700s to 1939.

caught in the 'visual amusements'
section in the basement, where there is
an intriguing collection of early
optical and theatrical toys. There are
model theatres ranging from simple
cardboard ones to those with elaborate
scenery, detailed figures and movable
properties. One is set up for a play,
The Yellow Dwarf, and dated about
1868. There is also a fine set of glove
puppets of Cinderella and the Ugly
Sisters, Charles II and two burglars.
The earliest optical toy was the
peepshow, dating from the eighteenth
century, of which there are several
examples; and there are also a shadow
theatre and a real Punch-and-Judy
booth, used by Mr Gus Wood from
1912 to 1962.

Visitors can stroll through two
centuries of children's costumes,
dating from the 1700s to 1939.
Exhibits, showing silk embroidery,
illustrate the history of the once-
thriving Spitalfields silk industry.
One of the primary collections in the
museum is the range of wedding
dresses worn in the nineteenth and
twentieth centuries. A special feature,
'The Creation of a Wedding Dress',
describes how the present Duchess of
Kent's dress was produced, and
includes sketches by the designer,
John Cavanagh, and a sample of the
finished work. Nearby is a fine
collection of workboxes, beautifully
inlaid, in coloured straw-work or
carved in wood.
Augmenting the costume collection
are many dolls of various
nationalities, designs and fashions.

The museum has the best-documented and most comprehensive range of dolls in the country, and also an impressive collection of dolls' houses in exquisite detail, the earliest of which was made in Nuremberg in 1673.

There is a gallery devoted to nineteenth century Continental decorative arts, and a historical collection of toys includes rocking-horses, model railways, buses and trams, and a host of parlour games — many from the Victorian and Edwardian eras.

Two remarkable exhibits are the models of Chinese rock gardens made of wood, ivory, pearl shell, enamel and kingfisher, which formed part of a gift from the Emperor of China to Napoleon Buonaparte's wife, Josephine. The ship taking them to France was captured by the British, whose subsequent offer to return them was rejected by Napoleon.

The museum building is itself a museum piece. Its unusual roof design is the best surviving example of the kind of prefabricated iron and glass construction that was used for the Crystal Palace and other Victorian buildings.

Practical details: Open from Monday to Thursday, and on Saturday, from 10 am to 6 pm. On Sunday it is open from 2.30 to 6 pm, and it is closed on Friday. The museum's art room is open, for the use of children, on Saturdays from 10.30 am to 12.30 pm and from 2 to 4 pm. Free admission. Nearest British Rail station is Cambridge Heath (ER), and nearest Underground station is Bethnal Green. Use buses 6, 6A, 8, 8A, 35, 55, 106 or 253.

Address: Cambridge Heath Road E2 9PA. Telephone (01) 980 2415.

THE BRITISH MUSEUM (AND BRITISH LIBRARY)

The biggest collection of antiquities in Britain

An Aladdin's cave of works of art from ancient kingdoms and cultures, and treasures found beneath our feet . . .

Behind the great classical facade of the British Museum lies the biggest collection of antiquities, printed books and manuscripts and *objets d'art* in the British Isles. The museum has been aptly referred to as 'the biggest jackdaw's nest in history'. Certainly this feast of exhibits makes it impossible to absorb, in a single visit, all that this wonderful museum has on public display (and much is held in reserve); even after years of repeated visits there will always be something fresh to see.

The museum's collections are divided into a number of departments: Egyptian Antiquities; Western Asiatic Antiquities; British and Medieval Antiquities; Pre-historic and Romano-British Antiquities; Oriental Antiquities, Greek and Roman Antiquities; Prints and Drawings; Coins and Medals; and — administered by the British Library — Printed Books, Manuscripts and Oriental Manuscripts and Printed Books. Also Ethnography (see

Museum of Mankind, page 99).
For the average visitor, as distinct from the specialist, certain displays deserve to be seen on the first possible occasion. And a suitable start can be made with that anchor of English liberties, Magna Carta, versions of which are in the Manuscript Saloon to the right of the main entrance hall. Magna Carta, which curbed the king's excessive powers, sprang from the Articles of the Barons sealed by King John at Runnymede in 1215, and the museum has a draft and two of the only four existing copies of the charter: the other two are in Lincoln and Salisbury Cathedrals.

Lewis Carroll's hand-written earlier version of *Alice in Wonderland*, first called *Alice's Adventures Under Ground*, is here, with Carroll's own

---

Below: the famous Portland Vase.

quaint drawings; also a memorandum written by Sir Christopher Wren setting out his design for the Monument to the Great Fire of London.

Exquisite illumination characterizes the Lindisfarne Gospels, written in Latin in AD 698 in honour of St Cuthbert, Bishop of Lindisfarne. Their significance is that Lindisfarne, or Holy Island, off the Northumbrian coast, was the birthplace of English Christianity.

Another historic book, William Shakespeare's first folio, is in the adjacent King's Library. It was published in 1623, and half of its 36 plays were appearing in print for the first time.

In 1939 an important archaeological discovery was made at Sutton Hoo, Suffolk: the remains of a Saxon ship burial. It is now displayed in the Early Medieval Room. The timbers of the ship had long since vanished, but the bolts and rivets were still in position, as can be seen in a series of remarkable photographs of the excavation. The ship, 89 feet long, symbolized the transition from this life to the next. The treasure displayed inside includes jewellery fashioned in gold and garnets, weapons and silver bowls and drinking-horns, some of them restored. The richness of the treasures suggests a king or ruler of the seventh century.

In the adjoining gallery are the Lewis chessmen, a collection of 78 carvings in walrus ivory, found by a peasant in the Outer Hebrides in 1831. They were probably made in England or

---

Opposite: The spectacular face mask from the Sutton Hoo Saxon burial ship.

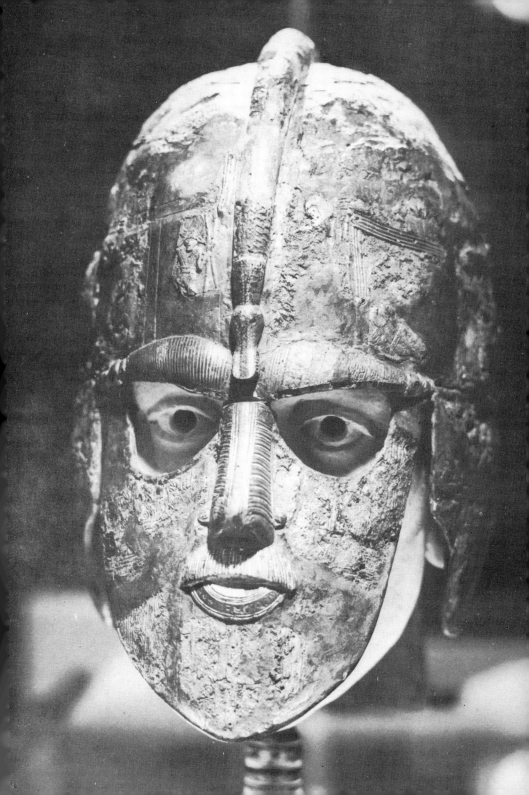

The Horse of Selene, part of the priceless Elgin Marbles.

Scandinavia in the early twelfth century, but whoever the carver was he had a nice sense of humour, judging by some of the facial expressions.

One of the museum's most recent and important acquisitions is the Savernake Horn, purchased for £210,000 in 1975, now kept in the Medieval Galleries. It is a medieval English hunting-horn, which takes its name from Savernake Forest, in Wiltshire, and is traditionally regarded as the horn of office of the hereditary Wardens of the Forest. The horn, made of ivory, is embellished with high quality silver-gilt and translucent-enamelled mounts depicting a king, bishop and a forester, animals and birds of the forest and heraldic lions.

From the Medieval Galleries go back down the main staircase to the Egyptian Sculpture Gallery and the famous Rosetta Stone. This large slab of black basalt bears one inscription in three scripts. It dates from 196 BC in the time of Ptolemy V and was found in the Nile Delta by one of Napoleon's officers. The Rosetta Stone's historical importance is inestimable, for the existence of Greek script on the Stone led experts directly to an understanding of Egyptian hieroglyphics, which also appear on it.

It was the capitulation of Napoleon's army in Egypt, and the surrender to the British of all that it had collected, that brought to the British Museum its first large sculpture. It now possesses the most complete Egyptian collection in the world except for the one in Cairo itself. Large sculptures of kings, gods and animals are arranged generally in order of date, and in the Egyptian rooms are mummies and mummy cases, coffins, and exhibits showing how the Egyptians lived.

Since 1962 the famous Elgin Marbles have had their own section known as the Duveen Gallery. The Marbles are a collection of sculptures from the Parthenon in Athens (others, from the Erechtheion, are in Room 9). They were bought by the British Government in 1816 from the Earl of Elgin, who was serving as British ambassador in Constantinople. Lord Elgin realized that the sculptures were rapidly deteriorating through neglect, and was allowed to bring them to England for safe keeping.

The Parthenon Marbles consist of metopes (panels which decorated the outer face of the temple, above the columns), relief slabs from the frieze, and sculptures from the pediments. The relief slabs of the frieze represent a ceremonial procession that took place in Athens every four years.

In the first Roman room stands, in splendid isolation, the Portland Vase, which despite its famed beauty has suffered a troubled history. This wonderful work of art (it may have been made by a Greek but it dates from the Roman period) is of opaque blue glass, with white figures in bas relief which are thought to represent the wooing of the sea goddess by Peleus. The vase dates from the first century AD and is only 9¾ inches high. It was found near Rome some time before 1600. Kept in the Barberini Palace until 1780, it was sold to the Scottish artist and antiquary James Byres. The British ambassador in Naples brought it to England in 1783, and the vase was then sold to the Duchess of Portland the following year. In 1810 it was lent to the British Museum, which bought it in 1945.

In 1845, disaster overtook the vase, when a visitor to the museum smashed it into more than 200 pieces. It was skilfully restored, but a large number of small fragments were left over. After World War II it was broken up again — this time officially — and restored once more, using modern cements and incorporating three of the 'surplus' pieces. Yet the Portland Vase remains an object of exquisite beauty.

In the Roman-Britain Room is a spectacular collection of fourth-century Roman silver plate found in Suffolk and declared treasure trove in 1946. There are 31 pieces in the Mildenhall treasure: platters, bowls, goblets and cutlery.

A valuable amenity offered by the museum to the public is its facsimile service, through which can be ordered plaster casts of almost any exhibit suitable for this type of copying. Prices are very reasonable. On a more limited scale, it also offers a range of replicas made in a tougher and more durable material, tinted or coloured to match the original.

Practical details: Open Monday to Saturday from 10 am to 5 pm, and on Sunday from 2.30 to 6 pm. Free admission. Nearby Underground stations are Tottenham Court Road and Holborn (Kingsway). Use buses 8, 14, 19, 22, 24, 25, 29, 38 or 73. Parking for disabled visitors only, by special arrangement. Refreshments available.

Address: Great Russell Street WC1B 3DG. Telephone (01) 636 1555 (for the Museum), and (01) 636 1544 (for the British Library).

BROOMFIELD MUSEUM

A northern retreat

Varied exhibitions of general interest in a parkland setting

Broomfield House stands in an attractive suburban park on the northern fringe of London. The house is probably of the seventeenth century, but has been much altered over the years. The half-timbering on the west front was only put on in the 1930s to stabilise the structure. The finest room is the entrance hall, with an early eighteenth-century fireplace and staircase, and murals probably painted by Gerrard Lanscroon.
There is a natural history room with a display of birds and animals found in the locality. The Westlake Room is used for exhibitions of paintings.

The rest of the museum is given over to a series of changing exhibitions of general interest.

Practical details: From Easter to the end of September opening hours are Tuesday to Friday from 10 am to 8 pm, and on Saturday and Sunday from 10 am to 6 pm. From October to Easter the Museum is open daily (except Monday) from 10 am to 5 pm. Free admission. Nearest British Rail station is Palmers Green (ER) and nearest Underground station is Arnos Grove. Use buses 29, 34, 102, 112, 123, 244, 251, 261, 298, 298A or W4. Easy parking. Set in open space. Refreshments available.
Address: Broomfield Park, Palmers Green N13 4HE.

BRUCE CASTLE MUSEUM

Where the postal service all started

Home of Sir Rowland Hill, who brought the sending of letters within reach of all

Bruce Castle is really three museums in one, each serving a different interest.
One section is devoted to postal history. This is appropriate because Bruce Castle was owned and occupied by the postal reformer and originator of the Prepaid Penny Post, Sir Rowland Hill, from 1827 to 1833. He was Secretary to the Post Office between 1854 and 1864. The building acquired its name from Robert Bruce, King of Scots, who at one time held the Manor of Tottenham.

Before Sir Rowland's major reform, postage cost four times as much, even for letters between neighbouring towns, and had to be paid by the recipient.

The museum's richest period for postal exhibits is 1700-1840, and features steam packet boats with original engravings, documents, a cutlass, powder horn and telescope.

The earliest postmen were called postboys, and highly disreputable some of them were. A postboy's riding boots, hat and whip can be seen. Delivering the post was at one time a hazardous occupation, and a newspaper of 1657 on show reports

The Royal Mail Coach — an early engraving by T. W. Huffam.

three highwaymen knocking down a postboy and stealing his mail, 'supposing it to be a Gentleman's Cloake Bagg'. There is a petition to Charles I from William Smith, postmaster at Oxford, referring to 'all sorts of discouragements, and some threatening no less than his life' for his service to the King during the Civil War.

Old newspapers, a collection of Victorian pillar-boxes and Victorian postmarks are among other exhibits of postal interest.

In the local history section are photographs and paintings of the area and there are many old documents: fourteenth-century Court Rolls, records of rentals in the time of Richard II, a baliff's account, grants of land and a shoemaker's bill.

RELICS OF A REGIMENT

'Die hard, my men, die hard!' This was the rallying cry at Albuhera, a Spanish village which saw the defeat of the French by the British during the Peninsular War in 1811. From then on the men of what was eventually to become the Middlesex Regiment were known as the 'Diehards'. An excellent collection of military relics is displayed on the first floor.

Drums, maces, medals, scarlet uniforms going back centuries make a colourful impact. In 1881 the regiment was titled the Duke of Cambridge's Own, and on display is the Duke's uniform, with baton, worn when he was Colonel-in-Chief from 1896-1904.

An interesting piece from World War II is part of the automatic multiple switchboard taken from Hitler's headquarters in East Prussia, labelled under the plug sockets with the names of the Fuehrer and other Nazi leaders, such as Himmler, Goering ('Reichmarshal'), Keitel and Bormann, Hitler's deputy.

The Middlesex Regiment was absorbed by the Queen's Regiment in 1967. It won 166 battle honours between 1790 and 1951 (Korea), and 11 of its men won the Victoria Cross.

Practical details: Open Monday to Friday (except Wednesday) from 10 am to 5 pm, and on Saturday from 10 am to 12.30 pm and from 1.30 to 5 pm. Free admission. Nearest British Rail station is Bruce Grove (ER) and the nearest Underground station is Wood Green. Use buses 123 or 243. Open spaces nearby. Easy parking.

Address: Lordship Lane, Tottenham N17 8NU. Telephone (01) 808 8772.

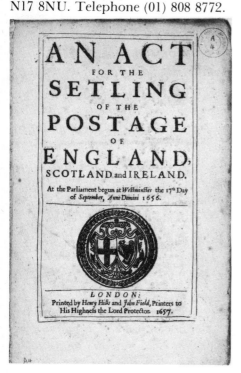

AN ACT
FOR THE
SETLING
OF THE
POSTAGE
OF
ENGLAND,
SCOTLAND and IRELAND.

At the Parliament begun at *Westminster* the 17th Day of *September, Anno Domini* 1656.

LONDON:
Printed by *Henry Hills* and *John Field*, Printers to His Highness the Lord Protector. **1657.**

Where Churchill planned the war

The secret subterranean 'nerve centre' of the second world war

Seventeen feet beneath Whitehall, in the basement of the building occupied by the Cabinet Office during the war, is a large network of rooms and passages. From here, the Prime Minister in effect ran the war.

Five of these rooms, protected from above by reinforced concrete and buttressed by heavy wooden beams, are preserved in detail. In the conference room, where Churchill and his War Cabinet met, the name cards on the table recall the luminaries of yesteryear: Attlee, Eden, Bevin, Ismay . . . Wartime 'utility' pencils still lie before their blotters. Maps of Europe and Italy deck the walls. Despatch boxes are to be seen, as if still awaiting their quota of documents. And should morale flag, there is Queen Victoria's injunction for all to see: *Please understand there is no depression in this house, and we are not interested in the possibilities of defeat. They do not exist.*

Along the corridor is a room marked simply 'Prime Minister' — Churchill's combined office, bedroom and air-raid shelter, as well as reception room. From the desk opposite his bed, still made up in a blue coverlet, he made many of his historic wartime broadcasts to the world. On the table nearby stands his cigar-cutter, given to him by an admirer, and on the wall are maps of Europe, with its pre-war borders, Northern Ireland and Britain, showing coastal defences, airfields and vulnerable beaches.

Outside in the corridor, steel helmets and gas-masks still hang on their pegs; a notice proclaims the schedule of air-raid alarm signals; 1939 telephone directories lie on a table opposite the tiny room from which Churchill had telephone conversations with President Roosevelt in Washington, their words being 'scrambled' unintelligibly to defeat any listeners-in.

Into the Map and Information Rooms, in the charge of senior Service officers, poured all information of possible value. Here it was sifted and distilled into reports for distribution to the Prime Minister and his Cabinet, to the Chiefs of Staff and their senior planners, and invariably to the King (the red box for the King's documents is still there). This room gave the Prime Minister an overall picture of the way the war was going on all fronts, the state of Britain's resources, industrial output, and the disposition of our forces throughout the world.

On the wall, maps covering all theatres of war are still stuck with pins and flags showing the positions of Allied and enemy armies, and the extent of the control zones in Germany after the European war was won.

There are records of flying bomb raids and casualties, and a three-dimensional, stereoscopic device for examining air photographs of bomb damage wrought by our aircraft over Germany. Information books compiled during the three years before

A wartime poster of Winston Churchill.

D-Day, give detailed profiles of, for example, Caen, Antwerp and Le Havre, often based on, and including, holiday snapshots of the invasion areas sent in by a helpful wartime public. Even a record of leave granted to personnel manning the War Rooms has been preserved.

Practical details: Visits take the form of free conducted tours and must be arranged in advance. Either write c/o 41, Sub-G, Treasury Chambers, Parliament Street, London SW1P 3AG, or telephone Mr C R Truter on (01) 233 8904 between 8.45 and 9.30 am only. The nearest Underground station is Westminster. Use buses 3, 11, 12, 24, 29, 53, 77 or 88.

Address: Whitehall SW1.

CARLYLE'S HOUSE

The home of one of London's greatest authors

A home frozen in time . . . where even the author's hat still hangs beside the door

Thomas Carlyle, author of the *French Revolution,* the monumental *History of Frederick the Great* and biographer of Schiller, lived in this house from 1834 until his death in 1881. Many were the famous who stepped across its threshold, including Dickens, Leigh Hunt (who lived nearby), Tennyson, Emerson and Browning. So well furnished is the house — most of the furniture here belonged to the Carlyles, together with books and pictures — that it is easy to imagine they were here only yesterday. Many possessions are still as Carlyle left them.

In the front dining-room is Mrs Jane Carlyle's armchair, and a picture by Robert Tait, *A Chelsea Interior,* hangs above the mantelpiece and shows the room exactly as it was in 1857. One day she was sitting in this chair when Leigh Hunt entered the room, and she jumped up and embraced him. Hunt was so impressed that he wrote a poem about it: *Jenny Kissed Me.*

Jane Carlyle's piano is also here, and it is thought that among those who played on it was Chopin — as he was a visitor here.

The library on the first floor is papered in William Morris's Willow Bough design, similar to the one here when Carlyle died. Formerly, this was Jane Carlyle's drawing-room, which she had enlarged in 1852.

No rooms are open on the second floor, but on the third is Carlyle's attic study, which he attempted in vain to insulate from the noise outside. Carlyle's writing desk, with its reflecting candle lamp, is still here, the well still stained with ink. On this desk he wrote all his books except *Schiller.*

Photographs can be seen showing Carlyle at work, and the house as it looked in his day. There are shelves filled with his books, and cases showing letters and manuscripts, his pen and inkstand. One of the most interesting pieces of correspondence was between Disraeli, when Prime Minister, and Carlyle. Disraeli, with gracious diffidence, offered Carlyle, in recognition of his work, a GCB (Knight of the Grand Cross of the Order of the Bath), and also the opportunity of receiving a life pension from the state. Carlyle proudly, but with equal grace, declined.

The basement kitchen is opening shortly, complete with range, pump, stone sink, dresser and scrub table.

Practical details: From March to October opening hours are Wednesday to Saturday from 11 am to 1 pm and 2 to 6 pm. Also Sunday from 2 to 6 pm. (The house closes at dusk if this is earlier.) During November, January and February it closes at 3.30 pm, and does not open at all in December. There is an admission charge. The nearest Underground station is Sloane Square. Use buses 11, 19, 22 or 49.

Address: 24 Cheyne Row SW3 5HL. Telephone (01) 352 7087.

Against all risks

Signs of the times when insurance first made its mark . . .

Besides stamping out the last vestiges of the Plague of 1665, the Great Fire of London (1666) brought with it one other benefit: it made people realize how vulnerable to disaster their property was, and prompted action to protect it. Hence the introduction of fire brigades, admittedly primitive at the time, and the formation of insurance companies which operated them.

The Chartered Insurance Institute possesses two impressive collections of several hundred British and foreign firemarks — plaques placed on the walls of all buildings insured by the companies against fire risk. Many of them are beautifully designed, and some are very early indeed, going back to the seventeenth century. There are two marks of the Friendly Society of London, which existed between 1683 and 1790, and a recently acquired collection of German firemarks.

On the second floor is the museum, with the accent strongly on firefighting. There is a fine frieze painting by C Walter Hodges representing the various principal forms of insurance — life, marine, fire and accident — with the Great Fire its main feature.

An early fire insurance plaque issued by Leeds Fire Office, 1777-1782.

Although the early firemen used land-based fire engines, they were in fact watermen working on barges, their firefighting duties being only part-time. A selection of the watermen's arm badges, mostly brass but some silver, fill one display case. Other exhibits include medals and awards, firemen's helmets (one of them, dated 1824, strongly resembling a top hat), and a collection of early insurance policies, from 1680 onwards.

To casual visitors, however, the star exhibits will doubtless be the three ancient fire engines. The earliest was owned by the Earl Winterton on his estate, Shillinglee Park, Sussex, in the eighteenth century. There is also one used in the parish of St Michael, Crooked Lane, City: its last outing was during the 850th anniversary celebrations of Bart's Hospital in 1973.

The first fire brigades were run by the insurance companies; and woe betide those who had no 'mark' on their houses.

A later, nineteenth-century fire pump, drawn by horses, is also on show. It was owned by the Royal Insurance Company.

Practical details: Open Monday. to Friday from 9.15 am to 5.15 pm. Free admission. Nearest British Rail station is Liverpool Street (ER). Nearby Underground stations are Mansion House, Moorgate and Bank. Use buses 6, 8, 11, 15, 22, 25 or 133. **Address:** 20 Aldermanbury EC2V 7HY. Telephone (01) 606 3835.

CHISWICK HOUSE

After the grand tour

Colour and splendour in the magnificent Roman manner

The Earl of Burlington, a leading patron of learning and the arts, had Chiswick House built to his own design in 1725. He had been influenced in choice of style, while on a Grand Tour, by the work of the Italian architect Palladio, who built in the magnificent Roman manner. And Chiswick is indeed magnificent. The external design was based on the Villa La-Rotunda at Vincenza by Palladio, and the Villa La-Rocca-Pisani by his apprentice Scammozzi, but the interior was the work of the architect and sculptor, William Kent. There are two floors, the higher one being loftier and more important than the lower, which housed the Earl's library and workrooms.

On the first floor the central feature is the Dome Saloon, a high octagonal room with pedimented doorways, busts and paintings. The dome itself has been restored to its original colourful splendour, the octagonal panels diminishing in size as they approach the dome's crown.

From the Dome Saloon other rooms branch off: the descriptively named Red, Blue, White and Green Rooms, the walls of each being covered in the appropriate colours. The Blue Room, one of the most decorated in the house, has a ceiling painting depicting Kent's conception of the Queen of Architecture.

Running the length of the villa is the gallery, which was intended as the setting for the Earl's art collection. Its small size is deceptive, for the illusion of spaciousness is heightened by vistas seen through arches, and its division into sections. The upper part of the room is richly gilded, as are the half-domes in the apses.

The garden was probably largely the work of Kent in co-operation with the poet Alexander Pope, who was England's first landscape gardener. The earliest garden of its kind, it is a paradise of vistas, statuary, temples and small bridges, features which reflected the desire at the time to engage the imagination as well as the eye.

Practical details: During April open daily from 9.30 am to 5.30 pm, and from May to September open daily from 9.30 am to 7 pm. In October and March open Wednesday to Sunday between 9.30 am and 5.30 pm, and from November to February open Wednesday to Sunday, 9.30 am to 4 pm. Closed daily from 1 to 2 pm all year round. There is an admission charge. Nearby Underground stations are Turnham Green and Hammersmith Broadway. Use buses 290 or E3. Easy parking near main entrance in Great West Road. Open space nearby. Refreshments available.

Address: Burlington Lane W4 2RS.

CITY OF LONDON POLICE MUSEUM

The tools of crime ~ and its prevention

Grim and gruesome weapons used in criminals' war on law and order

Just as the business of maintaining law and order is often a sombre task for the police, so the museum of the City of London Police, the oldest organized force in the country, has its grim side. The museum, arranged by a member of the City police, PC Donald Rumbelow, who has become an expert on London lore, offers a wide variety of reminders of the endless war on crime. A recent exhibit is a policeman's helmet crushed and broken by bomb blast. It was worn by PC Malcolm Hine, who miraculously escaped when a car bomb exploded outside the Old Bailey in 1973.

Years ago, in the early nineteenth century, truncheon-like tipstaffs were carried by the early policemen to identify the force to which they belonged. A selection of these, often colourfully decorated, is on show. Tipstaffs were basically symbols of office, and the surmounting crown unscrewed to disclose the arrest warrant, when necessary. When the tipstaff disappeared, decoration often continued on truncheons, also on display.

Early uniforms include an inspector's top hat of 1851 and greatcoat of 1863, and constables' uniforms of the 1880s.

The most notorious unsolved mysteries involving the City police were the Jack the Ripper murders in Whitechapel in 1888. The museum has photographs of one of the victims, Catherine Eddowes, found murdered in Mitre Square, and grisly viewing they make. There is also a photostat of a threatening letter, ostensibly from the murderer.

The last public execution was in 1868. There are death masks of two men who were hanged outside Newgate Prison, and an engraving of an execution of five pirates four years earlier. Leg irons and handcuffs from Newgate show the rather brutal means of restraint used in those days.

One of the most celebrated incidents in police history was the siege of Sidney Street, Houndsditch, and the museum has relics of the case. One night in December 1910, several men tried to rob a jeweller's shop. One of them, George Gardstein, was leader of the gang that shot dead three policemen; and that night he was himself accidentally shot by his own men. Two weeks later, two others in the gang were traced to 100 Sidney Street, which was besieged by police. (One of the spectators was Winston Churchill, then Home Secretary.) The house caught fire. One of the criminals was shot and the other suffocated to death in the smoke.

Among the exhibits is a model, made by a policeman at the time of the incident, of the jeweller's shop showing the position of the safe.

There are also pistols used by the gang and a poster bearing a portrait photograph of Gardstein after death, and offering a £500 reward for information leading to the capture of the others in the gang.

One case contains preserved specimens of a human heart showing the great damage caused by shotgun blast at close range; also an area of flesh with a stab wound, and two skulls damaged by iron bars. One unhappy man who wanted to make certain of his suicide contrived an elaborate wooden framework into which he fixed a double-barrelled shotgun, the muzzles aimed at the back of his neck. He tugged two cords, each of which was attached to a trigger. The device, which from the suicide's point of view was successful, is on display.

Weapons used for violent attacks are on show: a razor used by a Metropolitan Police officer, who was hanged for cutting his girl friend's throat; stones in socks, studded belts used as flails, knives, knuckledusters, pistols, and a deadly spring-loaded propelling pencil used as a gun.

Thanks to two officers, PCs Cross and Tibbs, whose duties in World War II included photography, there is a complete photographic record of every City air raid incident, including a panoramic view of the Barbican devastation. One exceptional picture, of a wall collapsing in Queen Victoria Street, has been published all over the world.

Practical details: The museum is not generally open to the public, but visits are occasionally arranged following written application to The Commissioner of Police for the City of London, Headquarters, 26 Old Jewry, London EC2R 8DJ. Nearby Underground stations are St Pauls and Barbican. Use buses 4, 8, 22, 25 or 141.
Address: Police Station, Wood Street EC2V 7HN.

CLOCKMAKERS' COMPANY MUSEUM

Where time stands still

Gas clocks, rolling-ball clocks, and those that tell moon phases and the position of the sun

Until about 600 years ago, people used water-clocks and crude sundials for telling the time. Then came mechanical escapement clocks which, in various forms, have been with us ever since. In Guildhall is a permanent exhibition of antique clocks and watches of the Worshipful Company of Clockmakers, which is believed to be the oldest of its kind in the world.

One of the first clocks to catch the eye is an astronomical striking clock in gilt-brass, made by Johannes Schneider of Augsburg in the early seventeenth century. Surmounted by figures of St George and the Dragon, it tells not only the time but the position of the sun, phases of the moon, and day of the year.

Another astronomical clock, slightly later in date, was owned by the scientist Sir Isaac Newton. The maker was Samuel Watson, the first Englishman to make elaborate clocks of this kind.

Two novel exhibits are worth close examination. In the early 1800s, William Congreve, who devised rockets for use in war, designed an interesting 'rolling ball' clock. A silver ball rolls slowly along a zigzag channel from one end of a rocking plate to the other, acting in place of a pendulum. In a year the little ball rolls 2,522 miles.

The other novelty is a nineteenth-century gas clock, which is 'wound' automatically by hydrogen released when a zinc ball falls into sulphuric acid.

There are scores of watches, watch keys, fobs and chatelaines, many of them beautifully jewelled and decorated, all demonstrating the best in the clockmaker's craftsmanship and art. Among the historic exhibits is a curious silver skull-shaped watch said to have belonged to Mary, Queen of Scots — a gift to her from a maid of honour.

One watch won its designer, John Harrison, a prize of £20,000 in 1765. For many years means had been sought which would calculate with certainty the longitude of a ship at sea. George III found that Harrison's watch gained a mere 4½ seconds in ten weeks, and its remarkable accuracy won him the prize.

The evolution of the watch is described in a display showing its progress between 1580 and 1884. But there is one interesting reminder of pre-clock days — a book dated 1659 called *The Universal Way of Dyalling*. It explains how to make and read a sundial, and was so popular that it was being reprinted as long after its first edition as 1805.

Practical details: Open Monday to Friday from 9.30 am to 5 pm. Free admission. Nearest British Rail station is Liverpool Street (ER). Nearby Underground stations are Bank, Moorgate and Mansion House. Use buses 6, 8, 11, 15, 22, 23, 25 or 133. **Address:** Guildhall, Basinghall Street EC2P 2EJ. Telephone (01) 606 3030.

The peoples of the Commonwealth

How people live and work in the British family of nations

A mass of national flags fluttering from a cluster of white flagpoles marks out unmistakably the Commonwealth Institute. This is a museum with a practical purpose: to give an insight into what the countries of the Commonwealth are like in environment and climate, how their peoples live and work, and what they make, grow and trade. The end products are greater co-operation and understanding between diverse peoples and nations.

Apart from adult members of the public, more than 100,000 school children a year visit the Institute's permanent exhibitions and take advantage of its excellent educational facilities.

Each country has its own display, and the wise visitor will not risk mental indigestion by trying to see too much at one go. The exhibitions are on three levels, and the exhibits vary widely in style of display.

Mauritius, for example, gives space to a splendid grouping of many kinds of coral; Nigeria shows a large detailed

Each nation has its own cultural display: the 'mudman' from Papua New Guinea.

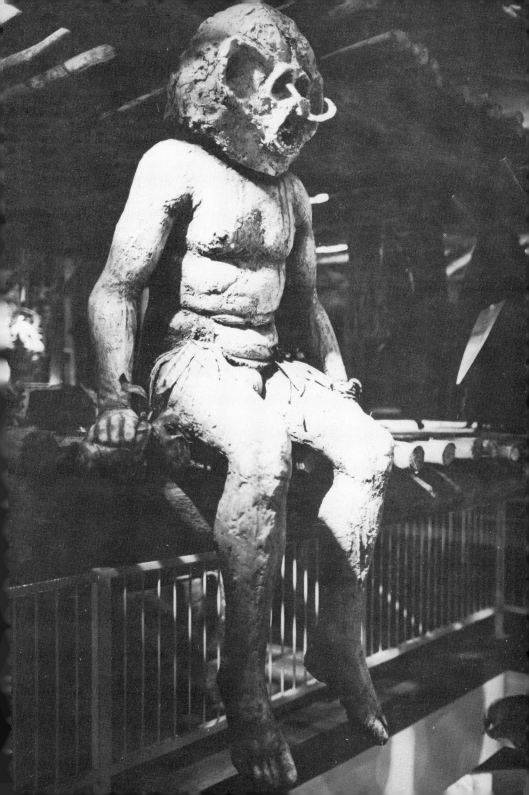

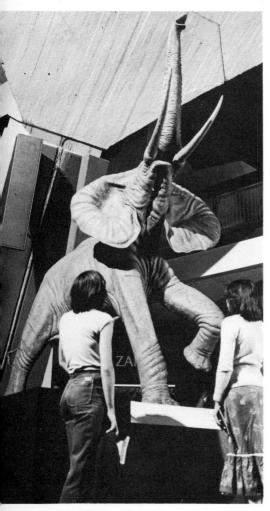

The animal exhibit from Nigeria.

model of an oil refinery, as well as colourful costumes, masks and carved dolls. Canada has an animated film, Malaysia a 'simulator' where visitors can experience this tropical land's heat and humidity.

Zambia strikes an individual note with a modelled group of a newly-born elephant being helped to its feet by older ones in the herd, and in contrast a three-dimensional representation of a copper mine. Papua New Guinea has an unnervingly lifelike model of a 'mudman'; Australia a 'talking construction engineer'.

Everywhere there are dioramas — illuminated three-dimensional models. New Zealand shows one of Auckland Harbour. India has a splendid series showing harvesting and processing sugar, cotton and tea. The Institute has a well-stocked book and general shop, and a library containing 40,000 books. Hundreds of periodicals of Commonwealth interest are regularly taken. Work books are distributed to children to encourage a study of the exhibits.

A large art gallery, with changing exhibitions of Commonwealth Art, and a cinema which doubles as a live theatre are also among the Institute's facilities. On Sunday afternoons in the autumn and winter, free entertainment by performers from different Commonwealth countries is a regular attraction.

The new building of the Institute was opened by the Queen, as Head of the Commonwealth, in 1962. It was given a truly international flavour from the start, for the highly individualistic building incorporates many materials — glass, rubber, timber and copper among them — donated by members of the Commonwealth 'family'.

Practical details: Open Monday to Saturday from 10 am to 5.30 pm, and on Sunday from 2.30 to 6 pm. Free admission. Nearest Underground station is High Street Kensington. Use buses 27, 28, 31, 49, 52 or 73. Easy parking. Refreshments available.

Address: Kensington High Street W8 6NQ. Telephone (01) 602 3252.

COURTAULD INSTITUTE GALLERIES

500 years of art

Paintings, glass and ivories spanning the centuries

This is a gem of an art gallery, not only for the high quality and range of its works — many of them world famous — but because of its compactness, excellent natural lighting and abundant seating.

The gallery opened in 1958. The original collection was the bequest to London University of Samuel Courtauld, the textile manufacturer and art collector, also of Viscount Lee of Fareham. These were augmented later by the bequests of Roger Fry, Sir Robert Witt and Mark Gambier-Parry.

Together, the works here span more than 500 years in the history of art. The Gambier-Parry collection is of fourteenth- and fifteenth-century Italian paintings, majolica ware, Venetian glass, ivories and enamels. The Lee collection of Old Masters includes Rubens's *Descent from the Cross*, which was probably the contract study for the central panel of the large altarpiece in Antwerp Cathedral, painted between 1611 and 1614. There are also works by Bellini, Botticelli, Cranach, Van Dyck, Gainsborough, Goya and Veronese. A number of famous French

Manet's 'Bar at the Folies Bergeres', one of many famous paintings at this gallery.

Van Gogh: Self Portrait.

Manet: Déjeuner sur l'Herbe.

Cézanne: The Card Players.

Renoir: La Loge.

Impressionist and post-Impressionist paintings distinguish the Courtauld collection, which includes Cézanne's *Card Players,* Manet's *Dejeuner sur l'herbe* and Renoir's captivating *La Loge,* and works by Degas, Pissarro, Monet, Sisley, Seurat, Van Gogh (including *Portrait of the Artist with his ear cut off),* Gauguin, Modigliani, Toulouse-Lautrec and Utrillo.

The Fry Collection offers pictures by Roger Fry and his circle, pottery and furniture from the Omega Workshop, founded by Fry in 1913, and paintings by his French contemporaries.

Practical details: Open Monday to Saturday from 10 am to 5 pm, and on Sunday from 2 to 5 pm. Free admission. Nearby Underground stations are Russell Square and Goodge Street. Use buses 14, 24, 29, 68, 73 or 134.

Address: Woburn Square WC1H 0NS. Telephone (01) 580 1015.

CRICKET MEMORIAL GALLERY

The Ashes

Here are the bats of cricket's 'greats', including WGG's — and The Ashes

In a small urn in this museum are the ashes of a wicket bail. They are *The Ashes*, traditionally (though not actually) won or lost in Test matches between England and Australia.

The Ashes, which never leave Lord's, passed into cricket history in 1882 when England, till then unbeaten on her own soil by Australia, lost a tense match by only seven runs. The *Sporting Times* mourned the sad event by running a mock obituary notice 'In affectionate remembrance of English cricket . . .', and announcing that 'the body would be cremated' and the ashes taken to Australia.

A little later, on a tour in Australia, the Honourable Ivo Bligh, captain, was presented with the ashes of a bail in a small urn by some ladies from Melbourne, and these are on display. Another memento of this historic tour is a batting order, scribbled with increasing feverishness during the match.

Among a host of cricketing relics are early photographs and paintings of international teams and individual players. One of these recalls the interesting fact that the first Australian cricket team to visit England (in 1868) consisted entirely of aborigines; white players were to wait another ten years.

Several pictures mark the course of early cricket. The oldest, nearly 300 years old, shows 'trap ball', an early forerunner of cricket.

The huge bearded countenance of that greatest of greats, W G Grace, is, of course, practically everywhere in one form or another. On show are the original sketches for the county cricket postage stamps of 1973 showing W G Grace's stances, and there are scores of original cartoon sketches of him garnered from many publications, including *Punch*. Also displayed are such relics as his snuff-box, the athletics medal he won in 1866, and the ball with which he scored his 100th century in 1895.

The evolution of cricket is illustrated by a collection of bats old and new, showing the changes in shape from the long, curved blade of around 1750 to the one used today.

Many of the famous names stare down at the visitor from picture and sculpture: Freddie Trueman in a large oil by Ruskin Spear; Sir Donald Bradman, painted in oil by R Hannaford; and Alec Bedser, perpetuated in a bronze statuette by David Wynne.

But perhaps the most bizarre exhibit is a bird — the celebrated sparrow which was struck by a fast ball bowled by Jehangir Khan of Cambridge University at Lord's on 3 July 1936.

Practical details: Open during the cricket season on match days — Monday to Saturday from 10.30 am to 5 pm. At other times by prior arrangement. There is an admission charge. Nearest Underground station is St John's Wood. Use buses 2, 2B, 6, 8, 16, 74 or 113. Easy parking. Refreshments available.

Address: Lord's Ground, St John's Wood Road NW8 8QN. Telephone (01) 289 1611.

Southwark in Roman times

Items from daily life in Southwark's historic past

Specializing in archaeological evidence for the history of the area, and in London superstitions, this museum contains finds from the large settlement established by the Romans in the middle of the first century on the south bank of the Thames where Southwark is today. Pottery and utensils are on show, with timbers from a Roman ship found in the locality. The museum is upstairs in Newington District Library building. Fragments of the medieval church which is now Southwark Cathedral, and three models of it illustrating subsequent developments, tell part of the story of medieval and post-medieval Southwark. There is also a model of a Jacobean theatre, like Shakespeare's Globe, which was a seventeenth-century feature of South Bank.

Pieces of seventeenth-century local delftware, and implements used in the nineteenth and twentieth centuries hop trade mark two of the area's once-thriving industries. There is a large stone sign which formerly identified the eighteenth-century Dog and Duck tavern, and a stuffed dancing bear which provided entertainment in the same period.

The huge iron pump from Marshalsea Prison, used in the eighteenth and nineteenth centuries by inmates who included Charles Dickens's impecunious parents, is on show, along with the tombstones of two notorious murderers, Frederick and Maria Manning, who were executed at Horsemonger Lane Gaol. Among the most interesting items from the last century are the experimental scientific instruments of Michael Faraday, the famous chemist and physicist, who was born at Newington Butts, near the Elephant and Castle, and made historic discoveries in the field of electricity. Strange superstitions of bygone days are recorded in the Lovett collection of such oddities as oak-apples worn as a necklace to ward off a sore throat, and a key attached to a hagstone — a stone with a hole in it — which was hung at the bedhead as a protection from nightmares and witches. There are several examples of household fittings with an acorn motif.

The oak tree was the mythical abode of the thunder god, and the acorn was considered a charm against lightning. The museum has several works by George Tinworth, a leading designer in Victorian and Edwardian times for Doulton's, whose potteries were in Lambeth until recent years: exhibits include two large terracotta reliefs, a model for a proposed Shakespeare memorial and a ceramic ornament.

Practical details: Open Monday, Tuesday, Wednesday and Friday from 10 am to 5.30 pm, on Thursday from 10 am to 7 pm, and on Saturday from 10 am to 5 pm. Free admission. Nearest Underground station is Elephant & Castle. Use buses 12, 35, 45, 68, 171 or 184.

Address: 155-157 Walworth Road SE17 1RS. Telephone (01) 703 3324/5529/6514, extension 32.

CUTTY SARK
AND GIPSY MOTH IV

The glory of sail

Close-up on two world-famous sailing ships, new and old

Three tall masts rising with stately grace above Greenwich and strung with skeins of rigging announce the *Cutty Sark*, the famous clipper, built in 1869, which has rested here in retirement since 1954.

Cutty Sark was built as a tea clipper, but was later employed in the Australian wool trade.

The weather deck is a good vantage point for seeing the complexity of rigging (ten miles of it, all told) which was manipulated by the crew, never more than 28 strong, to control the 32,000 square feet of canvas sails. On the bulwarks, coloured labels identify which rope controlled which sail.

A thorough tour of the ship can be made, taking in the poop deck (the sailing-ship equivalent of a steamship's bridge) where the captain stood and where the ship's wheel and compass are; the officer's quarters; the fo'c'sle (the cramped quarters where the crew lived); the galley (or kitchen), and the after deck-house, with its two lifeboats and 'jolly boat'.

In the upper cargo hold is a display of navigational instruments such as were used in the *Cutty Sark*. There are many models and other relics, which form part of the 'Long' John Silver collection. Near the entrance to this deck is the original figurehead of the *Cutty Sark,* and the sign, cut in metal, which adorned a masthead (a 'cutty sark' is a kind of short chemise). In the lower cargo hold is an outstanding display of colourful painted figureheads which once decorated the prows of nineteenth-century sailing ships.

The *Cutty Sark* carried tea from China from 1870 to 1877. Her fastest time for completing the voyage to England was 107 days. Between 1883 and 1895 she carried wool from Australia, and made the trip to England via Cape Horn in 73 days.

GIPSY MOTH IV

Only a few yards from the *Cutty Sark* is berthed the ship which tried to emulate her — the smaller, but equally distinguished 54-foot ketch *Gipsy Moth IV,* in which Sir Francis Chichester sailed single-handed round the world in 1966-7.

Visitors can quickly see the ingenious way in which Chichester was able to save himself time, trouble — and crew. The navigator's bunk, for example, was so placed that he could see the instrument dials while lying in it.

Practical details: Both ships are open Monday to Saturday from 11 am to 5.30 pm, and on Sunday from 2.30 to 5.30 pm (closing at 4.30 pm in winter). There is an admission charge to each, and children must be accompanied by an adult. Nearby British Rail stations are Greenwich (SR) and Maze Hill (SR). Use buses 108B or 177.

Address: Greenwich Pier SE10 9BL. Telephone (01) 858 3445.

THE DICKENS HOUSE MUSEUM

Discovering the world of Charles Dickens

Scene of both triumph and tragedy, the only surviving home of Charles Dickens

Charles Dickens lived in many houses in London, but this is the only survivor. It was the setting of happiness, achievement and one tragedy.

Dickens moved here with his wife and baby son, Charles, in 1837, and on 2nd April celebrated his first wedding anniversary. A week later came the publication of the first monthly issue of *Pickwick Papers,* and a dinner was given for him by his publishers. The family tragedy occurred a few weeks later, when 17-year-old Mary Hogarth, younger sister of Dickens's wife Catherine, suddenly died. Mary much admired Dickens and was much admired by him. 'She has been the grace and life of our home', he wrote sadly.

Although Dickens lived in Doughty Street for less than three years at the start of his literary career, the house is crowded with mementoes drawn from all periods of his life: letters, first editions, manuscripts and furniture, including the grandfather clock that

Dickens completed three books at Doughty Street: Pickwick Papers, Oliver Twist and Nicholas Nickleby.

belonged to Mr Pickwick of Bath, whose name Dickens borrowed for his immortal character.

Pictures and illustrations are everywhere. Lining the corridors and stairs are many original watercolours of Dickens characters by Frederick Barnard.

Dickens's ghost seems to accompany the visitor from room to room. Here in the small room at the back of the first floor is the desk he used at a later home, Gad's Hill, near Rochester. He completed *Pickwick Papers* in this room, and also wrote *Oliver Twist* and *Nicholas Nickleby* here.

There are original items of great interest to lovers of *Nickleby:* for example, a letter from the author in 1838 commenting on the brutality of one William Shaw — the supposed original of Mr Squeers, cruel headmaster of Dotheboys Hall in Yorkshire. Also on show is an advertisement inserted by Shaw in *The Times* in 1829 ('Youth are carefully instructed . . .'). Poor persecuted Smike is thought to have been inspired by the grave of George Ashton Taylor, at Bowes, the real-life setting for Dotheboys Hall.

On the second floor are books used by Dickens for readings from his own works, with stage directions and interpolations in the margins — helpful 'asides' like 'Ha, ha, ha' and 'Murder coming' in the reading of 'Sikes and Nancy'. Nearby is the specially made velvet-covered reading desk, which he gave to his daughter in 1870 after his last reading.

Dickens was, of course, the first editor — and a remarkably short-lived one, lasting only a matter of weeks — of the *Daily News*, which he founded in 1846, and there are pages from the paper on view.

In Mary Hogarth's second-floor room, the whole of one wall is filled with a painted backdrop for a play, Wilkie Collins' melodrama *The Lighthouse,* which hung originally at Gad's Hill. The play was produced by Dickens, an enthusiast of the amateur stage.

Something of the flavour of Pickwickian life is captured in the basement of Dickens House, where a reproduction kitchen is set out in the manner of Manor Farm, Dingley Dell. Other basement rooms are much as they were in Dickens's day.

Dickens's china monkey 'mascot', that he insisted on keeping on his desk beside him, is also on show, with a blacking pot of the kind he labelled when he worked in a warehouse, and a copy of *David Copperfield,* which members of the Scott Antarctic Expedition of 1912-13 took with them.

In two upper rooms are the exhibits from the Dickensiana garnered over the years by the late Comte Alain de Suzannet, an avid collector and admirer, who died in 1950. His gift to the house includes portraits of Dickens and many original drawings by Dickens's illustrators, including Seymour, Leech, Clarkson Stanfield (who painted *The Lighthouse* backdrop), 'Phiz' (H K Browne) and Marcus Stone.

Practical details: Open Monday to Saturday from 10 am to 5 pm. There is an admission charge. Parties by arrangement. Nearby British Rail stations are King's Cross (ER), Euston (LMR) and St Pancras (ER). Nearby Underground stations are Russell Square and King's Cross. Use buses 19, 38, 55, 171 or 172.

Address: 48 Doughty Street WC1N 2LF. Telephone (01) 405 2127.

DR JOHNSON'S HOUSE

Man of many words

Where Dr Johnson compiled his famous dictionary — the first of its kind

Dr Samuel Johnson, the great author, critic and dictionary compiler, lived in several houses in London, but only his Gough Square house survives. He was here from 1749 to 1759, and died in a house in Bolt Court only 50 yards away. But to admirers of Dr Johnson, this house is of special importance, for it was here that he compiled the famous dictionary which he was commissioned to produce by a syndicate of booksellers.

The two-volume first edition of the dictionary, published in 1755, is almost the first item encountered on entering the house. It lies on the dining-room table and can be inspected by visitors. There are about 800 copies of the first edition still in existence, and each costs between £1,000 and £1,500 to buy depending on its condition. Here there is an oil-sketch of Johnson by Barry, in which he is seen alert and animated.

In the parlour is a picture of the famous actor David Garrick. Johnson's attitude towards actors generally was not much above contempt, but Garrick was a pupil of Johnson's at his school near Lichfield, and he became a great friend. They originally came to London from Lichfield together at a time when Johnson was suffering harsh poverty.

Everywhere there are pictures of Dr Johnson's distinguished contemporaries: the painter Sir Joshua Reynolds, R B Sheridan, whom Johnson so much admired; and the Earl of Chesterfield. It was this ignoble lord who had led Johnson to expect his patronage and support, which did not manifest itself for seven years — until just before the dictionary was published — and only when it was assured of success. Johnson was understandably pained, and wrote accordingly in a famous letter to Chesterfield.

There is also a picture of James Boswell, who wrote the *Life of Johnson,* adjudged the greatest English biography of all time. Boswell, a barrister by profession, enjoyed mingling with the famous and recording their conversations; he became determined to write Johnson's life almost immediately when they first met in 1763. Boswell's crested drinking mug and coffee cup figure among a host of relics of Johnson and his circle displayed in two showcases.

The dictionary was compiled upstairs in the garret, which, restored after being badly damaged in World War II, can now be visited. Six clerks worked here on the dictionary, which took about eight years to produce. It was the first scientifically compiled work of its type, and is notable for the precision of its definitions and the many shades of meaning given.

Johnson was not without his prejudices, nor could he exclude his acid humour. Take, for example, his definition of 'Oats': 'A grain, which in England is generally given to horses, but in Scotland supports the people.' And his definition of 'Compliment': 'An act or expression of civility, usually understood to include some hypocrisy and to mean less than it declares.' The work remained the standard English dictionary for about a century.

The resident custodian of 17 Gough Square, which is owned by the Dr Johnson's House Trust, is Miss Margaret Eliot, who is extremely knowledgeable about Johnson and the house and will willingly answer visitors' questions.

Practical details: Open Monday to Saturday. In May to September from 11.30 am to 5.30 pm, and in October to April from 11 am to 5 pm. There is an admission charge. Nearby Underground stations are Blackfriars and Chancery Lane. Use buses 6, 8, 9, 11, 15, 22 or 25.

Address: 17 Gough Square EC4A 3DE. Telephone (01) 353 3745.

Portrait of Dr Johnson by James Barry (detail).

DULWICH COLLEGE GALLERY

Pictures in a country setting

Fine paintings in one of Britain's first public galleries

Built by Sir John Soane between 1812 and 1814, the Dulwich College Picture Gallery stands in an attractive semi-rural setting near the College.

It contains a fine permanent collection of English and European paintings. Especially noteworthy are Rembrandt's *Girl at a Window,* Watteau's *Le Bal Champêtre,* Poussin's *The Nurture of Jupiter,* and Di Cosimo's *Portrait of a Young Man.* Other artists represented include Canaletto, Claude, Cuyp, Gainsborough, Guercino, Hobbema, Hogarth, Kneller, Lely, Murillo, Raphael, Tiepolo, Reynolds, Rubens, Ruysdael, Van Dyck and Veronese.

Practical details: Open from Tuesday to Saturday: from May to August, 10 am to 6 pm; from September to October 15th 10 am to 5 pm; from October 16th to March 15th, 10 am to 4 pm; from March 16th to April 30th, 10 am to 5 pm. Also open on Sundays: from May to August, 2 to 6 pm; from April to September, 2 to 5 pm. There is an admission charge.

Nearest British Rail stations are West Dulwich (SR) from Victoria, and North Dulwich (SR) from London Bridge. Use buses 3, 12 or 37.

Address: College Road SE21 7LD. Telephone (01) 693 5254.

Queen Elizabeth's hunting lodge

Close-up on the natural history of London's historic 'back garden'

This handsome timber-framed building dates from about 1500, and has strong associations with hunting and its royal patron, Elizabeth I. The house was in fact a grandstand, built to view the hunt on Chingford Plain. Here, it is said, Elizabeth heard the news of the Spanish Armada's defeat in 1588.

Enjoying wide views of Epping Forest, the Lodge is a fitting home for the museum, with its emphasis on wild-life, conservation and local archaeology. The many instructive displays feature mammals, animal tracks, butterflies and birds, insects, and trees and flowers.

Displays of badger, fox and their families are accompanied by relics formerly the property of the old forest keepers (the Lodge was occupied by a forest keeper from the 1660s to the 1920s). Other exhibits include squirrels, a hare, a rabbit, a water-rat and a hedgehog — and deer (deer are now rarely seen in the forest). Children especially will be interested in a series of preserved foetuses demonstrating the development of a deer before birth.

Also worth seeking out is the beautifully engraved invitation to Queen Victoria to open the forest to the public in 1882.

Practical details: Open Wednesday to Sunday from 2 to 6 pm (closing at dusk in winter). There is an admission charge. School visits by arrangement. Nearest British Rail station is Chingford (ER). Use buses 69, 102, 179 or 242. Easy parking. Open spaces nearby. Refreshments available.

Address: Rangers Road, Chingford E4 7QH. Telephone (01) 529 6681.

The museum is now associated with the Epping Forest Conservation Centre at High Beach, two or three miles away, which was opened in 1971. The day centre is managed by the Field Studies Council and is expertly staffed and equipped with teaching laboratories, lecture theatre, library, information desk and a permanent exhibition about the Forest.

Practical details: The information desk and display area are open from Wednesday to Saturday, 10 am to 12.30 pm and 2 to 5 pm. Also on Sunday from 11 am to 12.30 pm and 2 to 5 pm. Educational visits must be booked in advance.

Address: High Beach, nr Loughton, Essex. Telephone (01) 508 7714.

FARADAY MUSEUM AND LABORATORY

One of the founders of modern science

This is where one of the world's greatest scientists made his momentous discoveries

When young Michael Faraday was apprenticed to a bookbinder, he began to read the books he bound, became interested in science and so impressed Sir Humphry Davy, head of the Royal Institution, that he was taken on as Davy's assistant. Thus began a career of research in electricity and magnetism which was to yield up discoveries of profound importance to the world.

Faraday's original laboratory still exists, in the basement of that seat of scientific learning, the Royal Institution. It is the major feature of the Faraday Museum and was restored in 1973 to its original form. It was opened by the Queen using Faraday's original electromagnetic induction coil to part the curtains which covered the commemorative plaque.

Faraday's equipment is arranged in the laboratory as if for an experiment involving the use of his great horseshoe electromagnet. Jars of chemicals fill the surrounding shelves. On a table nearby a notebook used to record his experiments (16,000 are described) lies open as if for the next entry. It is just as if Faraday were about to enter the room and carry on

Faraday's magnetic laboratory, where he made his most momentous discoveries, including the world's first transformer and the first dynamo.

where he left off...

It was in this small laboratory, with one assistant and on a salary of £100 a year, that Faraday made his most momentous discoveries. He made a simple device using a bowl of mercury, a magnet and a suspended wire which constituted the first electric motor. Later came the first transformer and the first dynamo. Actual and reconstructed equipment demonstrating these are in the museum, along with Faraday's Ring — the device with which he discovered electromagnetic induction — and the cylinder machine made by Faraday when a bookbinder's apprentice.

Tireless scientist that he was, Faraday also worked in other fields from time to time. He experimented to improve optical glass, discovered benzene, developed new alloys of steel (many of which were too far ahead of their time to be of value). Examples of the glass and metals are on show, also a razor, penknife and a sword. There is also the great cylinder machine used by Davy and later in 1836 by Faraday in investigations into the nature of electrical discharge.

There are glass cases displaying his diaries of experiments and the handwritten, bound collection of reports of four lectures by Davy which Faraday gave Davy in his apprenticeship days. Personal possessions there include his spectacles, tinder-box, portable microscope and travelling case, also some of the many medals and orders from various countries, including France, Denmark and Prussia, in recognition of his work.

Although he accepted many honours from British learned and scientific societies, Faraday was basically a modest man. He turned down the offer of a knighthood at least once, contenting himself with his role as Superintendent of Laboratories at the Royal Institution and the academic distinction of Fullerian Professor of Chemistry. With him, science came first and last.

Practical details: Open only on Tuesday and Thursday, from 1 to 4 pm. There is an admission charge. Nearby Underground stations are Green Park and Piccadilly Circus. Use buses 14, 19, 22 or 38.
Address: Royal Institution, 21 Albemarle Street W1X 4BS. Telephone (01) 409 2992.

A fine collection of porcelain

Collections of porcelain, antique keyboard instruments and paintings

The date 1693 was found scratched on a brick in a chimney-stack at this spacious house, and this is taken to be when it was probably built. After passing through many ownerships since the William and Mary days, Fenton House was bought in 1936 by Lady Binning, who died in 1952 and bequeathed it to the National Trust, the present owners.

Fenton House contains two remarkable collections which can be seen by the public. With the house Lady Binning left one of the most impressive private collections of eighteenth-century European porcelain, much of it English. The cream of the English collection is in the left alcove of the Porcelain Room. The comprehensive range of Continental porcelain has a strong element of Meissen, and in the Oriental Room, European porcelain's great debt to its originators, the Chinese, is fully acknowledged. In the drawing-room there is a beautiful pink-scale Worcester hexagonal vase and cover, considered the most important item in the English porcelain group.

In contrast is a collection of more than a dozen keyboard musical

instruments, presented to the National Trust in 1937 by the late Major George Henry Benton-Fletcher. It consists of a number of harpsichords, and the harpsichord's smaller cousins, the virginals and spinets, are also represented, many of them exquisitely painted or inlaid. Unlike those of the piano, harpsichord and spinet strings are plucked, not struck with hammers, but there is also a clavichord on display, the action of which is similar to a piano's. The instruments are maintained in playing condition: public recitals are frequently given, and serious students are permitted to practise on them.

The oldest instrument is in the Rockingham Room — a five-sided

Part of the impressive collection of European and Chinese porcelain at Fenton House.

Italian spinet dated 1540. It is of cypress wood.

The house has an attractive walled garden, which is free to the public when the house is open.

Practical details: Open Wednesday to Saturday from 11 am to 5 pm, and on Sunday from 2 to 5 pm. Closed throughout December, and open only at the weekend in January and February. There is an admission charge. Nearest Underground station is Hampstead Heath. Use buses 24, 46, 210 or 268.

Address: Hampstead Grove NW3 6RT. Telephone (01) 435 3471.

FORTY HALL

A former Lord Mayor's home

A parkland museum in the Lea Valley

This fine Jacobean house, built in the style of Inigo Jones, is situated in what once formed part of the Forest of Middlesex. It was completed in 1632 for Sir Nicholas Raynton, a rich haberdasher who became Lord Mayor of London.

The house provides a tasteful setting for changing exhibitions, containing some attractive period furniture, including two mid-seventeenth-century lacquered cabinets; eighteenth-century table glass; needlework and porcelain. There are a number of paintings, water-colours, prints and drawings, one attributed to John Constable, and another by Thomas Rowlandson (1756-1827) who frequently visited this area, and some old maps of Hertfordshire and Middlesex.

Sir Nicholas Raynton is himself the subject of a portrait by William Dobson (1643). There is a painting of a young Flemish woman by Lucas de Heere (1568), and an excellent oil of Henrietta Anne, daughter of Charles I, by Jan Mytens (1661), in a beautiful inlaid frame.

There are also displays of medieval 'finds', many of them locally excavated.

The pleasant parkland in which the house stands offers a fine view across the Lea Valley. To the east of the house is a vast Cedar of Lebanon, thought to be nearly 300 years old. The evergreen magnolia, next to the south door, dates from 1850.

Practical details: Open from Easter to September, Tuesday to Friday, 10 am to 8 pm, and Saturday and Sunday from 10 am to 6 pm. From October to Easter, 10 am to 5 pm (or park closing time if earlier) daily except Monday. Free admission. Nearest British Rail stations are Enfield Town and Enfield Chase (ER). Use buses 135, 231, 217, 217B or W8. Easy parking. Open space nearby.

Address: Forty Hill, Enfield EN2 9HA. Telephone (01) 363 8196.

Life down the centuries

Three hundred years of living-rooms and furniture, shops and doorways

In many stately homes one can step back into the past and taste a single period of history in often-luxurious detail; the Geffrye Museum, however, gives an insight into how a middle-class family would have lived during three centuries.

Furniture is the main theme here, in what was originally a terrace of almshouses erected under the will of Sir Robert Geffrye, Lord Mayor of London in 1685.

The almshouses now form a continuous corridor of rooms, each authentically furnished and decorated according to a specific period. In the Geffrye Museum, time begins around the year 1600. In the entrance hall are Georgian shop-fronts and doorways preserved from eighteenth-century London. Near by is a woodworker's shop, with tools of the period set out on the craftsman's bench, with such devices as a foot-operated pole lathe.

The first room is an open hearth kitchen complete with spits, iron cooking pots and many other utensils. On the dresser is a sugar loaf, which had to be cut into pieces with tongs. The display demonstrates the important part played by craftsmanship in the manufacture of vessels and implements.

The Elizabethan Room, complete with woven matting on the floor, a cradle, beautifully carved oak chests and a magnificent oak mantelpiece, shows the development of panelling from Tudor to Jacobean styles.

Beside each room are detailed descriptions of particular items of interest in word and picture. Thus as complete an impression as possible is given of domestic life in bygone days.

Moving through the Stuart Room (in the style of Sir Christopher Wren), and the William and Mary Rooms, one can discern the increasing gracefulness and prosperity of home surroundings; though personal habits, as we are reminded, were often crude.

Along the corridor is the almshouses' original chapel, itself demonstrating the simplicity of the eighteenth century. The lettered panels bearing the Creed and Commandments were uncovered during restoration work as recently as 1971.

Many of the rooms' features were taken from real houses: the pine panelling in the Early Georgian Room, for example, came from a house in Chancery Lane, and the chimneypiece from another in Putney; in the Late Georgian Room, more panelling, this time from a house in Aldgate.

The mid-Victorian Room is furnished in the style of the 1850s — about the time of the Great Exhibition. Collectors and antique-shop browsers will be on familiar ground here, looking at dried flowers under glass domes, gilded mirrors, firescreens — and a spittoon, a by no means uncommon 'adornment' of Victorian living-rooms.

In the Voysey Room, largely devoted to products designed by C F A Voysey, who rebelled against Victorian styles, are furniture and equipment of the early twentieth century, including a contemporary telephone and a phonograph, the cylindered forerunner of the modern gramophone and record player. Coinciding with the museum's Diamond Jubilee in April 1974, two new rooms showing two distinct styles of domestic design in the 1930s were opened in the south wing, above the exhibition hall. One shows a typical suburban 'lounge' of the mid-1930s, in a form of Art Decor, the other a more tasteful living-room with individually designed furniture and carpet — an instructive contrast.

The museum is augmenting its art collection illustrating costume and social life, and among pictures recently acquired are *Londoners Gypsying* by C R Leslie (1820), two scenes of children playing games by Harry Brooker (1890/91), and in the William and Mary Room, an important discovery — *Self-portrait with her husband Charles and their son Bartholomew* by Mary Beale (1663/64).

In the north wing are work rooms for children, which are also open to interested visitors. Here, by arrangement, children may dress up in reproduction period costume, using one another as models for painting.

Practical details: Open Tuesday to Saturday from 10 am to 5 pm, and on Sunday from 2 to 5 pm. Free admission. Nearest British Rail *and* Underground stations are Liverpool Street (ER) and Old Street (ER). Use buses 22, 22A, 48, 67 or 149. Easy parking. Open space nearby. Refreshments available.

Address: Kingsland Road, Shoreditch E2 8EA. Telephone (01) 739 8368.

GEOLOGICAL MUSEUM

A storehouse of gems and jewels

Precious stones, moon rock and fossils feature in spectacular exhibitions telling the Earth's turbulent story

Though the Geological Museum is not one of the biggest of the national museums, a visit is certain to be rewarding. Where else, for example, could one see such a profusion of precious and semi-precious stones under one roof?

This rich and colourful collection is among the first to be seen on entering the museum's main hall. Illuminated cases with non-reflective glass show the stones in their raw natural state and at various stages in cutting. The diamond case contains models of the Koh-i-noor and other large and famous gems; it also shows the industrial use of diamonds, and a number are to be seen set around the rim of a bit used for rock-drilling. There are beautiful examples, cut and uncut, of topaz, garnet, zircon, jade, jasper, agate and amethyst. Perhaps the most impressive is the opal case, with its fine range of stones of varying degrees of milkiness and luminosity. Rearing up at the back of the hall is a giant rock face 25 feet high — in fact a completely convincing replica of a cliff near Loch Eilt in Inverness-shire. It was ingeniously copied by a team of students, directed by a sculptor, James Turner, in December 1971. The technique they used is described in

detail in words and photographs alongside, but briefly it involved laying a flexible skin mould over the real rocks. The mould was then transported to London, hung up in the museum, and layers of special plaster applied to it. It was then realistically painted by Patricia Turner, the sculptor's wife.

The rock forms the imposing entrance to the elaborate permanent

Moon rock from the Apollo 16 space mission, in the Geological Museum.

exhibition, 'The Story of the Earth'. This describes the earth as a planet, its composition, how the solar system was formed and the origin of the continents and oceans. It uses illuminated diagrams and film as well as a star-scattered night sky on the curved ceiling. There are several animated exhibits, including a spectacular one showing lava pouring down the sides of an erupting volcano, and also an 'earthquake machine', which shakes and rumbles as you stand on it. Accompanying this are pictures of the devastating Alaskan earthquake of 1964.

Outside this exhibition is a geological globe of the earth, and large pieces of minerals such as quartz and fluorspar. There is also a six feet high stalagmite split down the centre: it came from Yugoslavia and was presented to the museum in 1906.

A solitary display case in the main hall shows, 'frozen' in a pyramid of transparent plastic, a fragment of white moon rock, brought back by astronauts on the Apollo 16 mission. It is nearly as old as the earth itself. There are many large and impressive fossils on show — a selection from the museum's vast stock of about a million specimens of fossils, rocks and minerals.

A new exhibition, 'Britain Before Man', is a helpful and easily understood curtain-raiser to the subject of geology and the Earth's progress through the 3,000 million turbulent years of its existence. It is explained by means of slide shows, colour photographs, dioramas and models. The story is told chronologically: The Beginning; The Dark Ages; The Era of Mud; Continent; Coral Seas; Coal Forests; and Baking Deserts and Tropical Seas. The exhibition concludes with a diorama on Man himself.

Another exhibition in this series will be 'British Fossils' in late 1979, and in 1981 a major new exhibition, 'Treasures of the Earth', will feature materials from the Earth's crust used by man in everyday life.

The main staircase up to the first-floor gallery is made of several different kinds of British marble. In this gallery are rock displays from eighteen regions of the British Isles, often with detailed relief models, maps and dioramas. Other exhibits include a large piece of glaciated pavement — a surface of bedrock over which a glacier has passed. Scratches from rocks at the bottom of the ice can be clearly seen in the bedrock. Some of the displays in this gallery show fossilized bones of prehistoric creatures, such as moose, mammoth, elephant and rhinoceros.

On the second floor, among the minerals, are models of large gold nuggets — one piece weighs 27½ pounds — and a range of metallic ores, including gold and silver, as well as base metals.

There is also a model of Stonehenge in its original complete shape. Geologists found that different kinds of stone were used for the circle, which was erected between 2000 and 1700 BC. The larger stones in the outer circle were found locally, but the smaller ones came from South Wales — 200 miles away. In all probability, they were brought on rafts, though one well-known geologist thinks they were carried in by ice during the Ice Age.

The Geological Museum offers regular programmes of lectures and films.

Practical details: Open Monday to Saturday from 10 am to 6 pm, and on Sunday from 2.30 to 6 pm. Free admission. Nearest Underground station is South Kensington. Use buses 14, 30, 49, 52, 73 or 74.

Address: Exhibition Road SW7 2DE. Telephone (01) 589 3444.

GOLDSMITHS' HALL

Over 650 years of the goldsmith's craft

Some of the finest work in gold and silver

The proud and venerable Worshipful Company of Goldsmiths has, since 1397, patronised and encouraged high standards for the art and craft of designing and fashioning articles from gold and silver.

By law, none must be sold unless it is assayed (tested) and approved by the London Assay Office or by one of the other three provincial Offices. The Company assays many thousands of items every day at Goldsmiths' Hall, rejecting those of sub-standard metal. Those of good quality are hallmarked with sponsor's mark, the standard mark, leopard's head and date letter. Visits to Goldsmiths' Hall are arranged through the City Information Office (see address below), which is notified when the Hall is available. In the Hall's sumptuous state rooms are displayed some of the Company's much-prized silver pieces. Much of it is used regularly: cutlery, plates, goblets, condiment sets, both old and new, appear on the tables at the Company's luncheons and dinners.

The present hall, the restored original work of Philip Hardwick, is the third to be built on this site. On the marble staircase in the entrance hall stands a gilded wooden statue of St Dunstan,

The Bowes Cup at Goldsmiths' Hall, said to have been used at the Coronation of Elizabeth I.

the goldsmiths' patron saint, himself a practitioner of the craft: the figure once adorned the Company's seventeenth-century barge. The four marble statues on the staircase are by Samuel Nixon and represent the

*A masterpiece in silver-gilt made by
Paul de Lamerie in 1741.*

four seasons.

The Livery Hall has a richly ornate
ceiling and five impressive crystal
chandeliers which were displayed at
the Great Exhibition of 1851. There
are oil paintings of the Prince
Consort, Queen Adelaide and Queen
Victoria.

Visitors may be shown a selection of
the finest pieces in the Hall's
collection, including a rococo-style
silver-gilt jug and large dish made by
Paul de Lamerie in 1741. The
Company, of which Lamerie was
thrice Warden, describes the dish as
the masterpiece of Britain's greatest
goldsmith. The dish was
commissioned to help replace plate
melted down during the Civil War and
the Great Fire of London and other,
later, troubles. In the centre, in relief,
is the Company's coat-of-arms, with
classical Roman figures, animals and
diaper work round the border.

In the adjacent Court Room is a
Roman stone altar to Diana. It was
unearthed in 1830 during preparatory
work for the present building. The
Drawing-Room, almost totally
destroyed in World War II, has several
attractions. The decor reproduces
Louis XVI style, there are a musical
bracket clock by George Clarke and
two seventeenth-century Brussels
tapestries by Le Clerc.

Several of the Goldsmiths' earliest and
most beautiful treasures may be
displayed in the Exhibition Room.
The Royal Tudor Clock Salt (c 1530)
was one of several items earmarked, at
the Tower of London, for melting
down after Charles I's execution. A Mr
Smith offered £43 for it — and saved
the piece from extinction.

The Bowes Cup, presented to the
Company by Sir Martin Bowes, a
former Lord Mayor and 13 times
Prime Warden, is said to have been
used by Elizabeth I at her Coronation
banquet in 1558.

The Seymour Salt (c 1662) is thought
to have been given to Catherine of
Braganza when she arrived in England
to marry Charles II. Samuel Pepys
called it 'one of the neatest pieces of
plate that I ever saw'. It was a gift to
the Company from a liveryman who
in 1693 sought to excuse himself from
what he feared would be an over-
exhausting tour of duty as
Touchwarden.

It is emphasised that members of the
public may not see all the items
mentioned, as the display is changed
constantly.

Practical details: Visits must be
arranged with the City of London
Information Centre, St Paul's
Churchyard EC4. Their telephone
number is (01) 606 3030. Nearest
Underground station to Goldsmiths'
Hall is St Paul's. Use buses 8, 22 or 25.

Address: Foster Lane EC2V 7AA.

GUNNERSBURY PARK MUSEUM

Early hansom cabs and coaches

The home of the Rothschilds, and horse-drawn cabs that once rattled through London's streets

Situated in an attractive public park, Gunnersbury Park House is now a museum housing the coaches once used by the Rothschild family and now skilfully restored.

The travelling chariot, solid and heavy for coping with the poor Continental roads, was built in the early 1800s. Four horses would normally have drawn this capacious coach, with a postillion mounted on one of them.

The town chariot, built in Wandsworth about 1820, has a platform at the back where two liveried footmen stood. The coach, which was used to travel between Gunnersbury and Park Lane, London, is tastefully painted in blue and yellow (the family colours) and the inside trim is blue silk damask and silk, and worsted 'lace'.

The third coach will be familiar to modern Londoners through cinema shots of nineteenth-century streets and swirling fog — the hansom cab, predecessor of the motor taxi. The hansom was invented by and named after Joseph A Hansom, who died in 1882. It was drawn by one horse, which had almost no weight to bear as the driver, standing at the rear, balanced the load.

Several other interesting vehicles here claim attention: a bath chair used by Baroness de Rothschild, a Humber tandem tricycle of 1880, a milk pram (c 1900), a late nineteenth-century pony trap and a manually operated fire-engine of 1890.

'Stone Age man and his tools' is the theme of another group of exhibits, the results of local excavations. Saxon and Viking weapons are also on show. The topographical material includes more than 2,000 prints, drawings, maps and photographs, a selection of which is always on show.

Practical details: Open April to September, Monday to Friday from 2 to 5 pm, and Saturday and Sunday from 2 to 6 pm. From October to March it is open daily from 2 to 4 pm. Free admission. Nearest Underground station is Acton Town. Use bus E3, or on summer Sundays and Bank Holidays, 15. Easy parking at Pope's Lane entrance. Open space nearby. Refreshments available in summer.

Address: Gunnersbury Park W3 8LQ. Telephone (01) 992 1612.

A Rothschild posting chariot used by the family for continental travel.

HAM HOUSE

House of splendour

A richly decorated and furnished country residence of the seventeenth century

Sir Thomas Vavasour, Knight Marshal to James I, built Ham House for himself in 1610, and great efforts have been made to restore it to its original splendour. Certain features have been added, for example the Great Staircase with its beautiful carved panelling, which was installed in 1637. The house was enlarged in the 1670s.

Most of the furniture here dates from the late seventeenth century, the period when it was owned by the Duke of Lauderdale, a minister of Charles II, and at its luxurious best.

The house is richly decorated and furnished, and contains many paintings. There is an excellent collections of inset pictures — a feature of the Restoration period — the best of which were painted by Willem van de Velde.

There are a number of portraits by Sir Peter Lely in the Long Gallery (and a fine one by him of Elizabeth Dysart as a young woman in the Round Gallery) and several by Sir Godfrey Kneller and John Vanderbank. Sir Joshua Reynolds is the creator of a full-length portrait of Charlotte Walpole, and there are two early pictures of other Countesses of Dysart after Reynolds and Hoppner by John Constable, who often stayed at Ham.

The Marble Dining-Room still has its seventeenth-century gilt-leather wall-covering. In a small room off the Round Gallery is an admirable display of miniatures, including one of Queen Elizabeth I by Nicholas Hillard. The ceiling painting in the White Closet is by Antonio Verrio, whose work can also be seen at Hampton Court Palace (see below). The bedroom over the chapel has been converted into a museum. Here are displayed a specimen of each of the sets of chairs in the house which still possess their original upholstery, and many textiles of the seventeenth century. In remarkable condition is a toilet set in rich Lyons silk with silver brocade, made at the time of the 4th Earl of Dysart's marriage in 1729, possibly as a luxury wedding gift. The Earl's robes as a Knight of the Thistle are also preserved here, and so is the original inventory of the house in 1679.

Practical details: Open from Tuesday to Saturday, in April to September from 2 to 6 pm and in October to March from 12 noon to 4 pm. There is an admission charge. Nearest British Rail *and* Underground station is Richmond(LMR). Use buses 65, 71, 90 or 90B. Easy parking at Ham Street entrance. Open space nearby. Refreshments available.

Address: Ham Street, Richmond TW10 7RS. Telephone (01) 940 1950.

Cardinal Wolsey's famous palace

Magnificent royal apartment, paintings, armoury, maze — and a ghost

Hampton Court Palace is a grand memorial to the power and affluence of Cardinal Wolsey, during the reign of Henry VIII, in the period 1514 to 1525. By 1529, Wolsey had been discredited and his property and goods were forfeited to the king, although in a vain attempt to mollify him Wolsey had already given the king Hampton Court. The king greatly enlarged the building, and of his six wives five were taken to live there. It was used by all monarchs until the death of George II in 1760.

The moat bridge, with the stone King's Beasts quaintly standing guard on either side, leads through the Great Gate into Base Court and beyond into Clock Court — so-called because above the second-floor window of Anne Boleyn's Gateway is the famous Astronomical Clock of 1540, now restored and re-painted in authentic colours. An interesting feature of the clock is that, at its centre, the sun is seen to revolve round the earth — in accordance with beliefs then current. In this court is the entrance to the State Rooms, which are in two suites, the

Hampton Court offers a lot to the visitor: the famous maze, the largest vine in England, and two hundred years of state apartments.

King's Side and the Queen's, each of which is reached by a state staircase. The walls and ceiling of the King's Staircase are covered by an elaborate mythological painting by the Italian artist Verrio. The King's Guardroom is notable for an impressive display of 3,000 arms of all kinds: guns, halberds and swords, set in the pattern designed by William III's gunsmith.

In many of the rooms are displayed paintings from the Royal Collection, including works by Tintoretto, Titian, Correggio and Brueghel.

The Queen's Gallery is a fine 80-foot-long room, decorated with tapestries made in 1662, and large blue and white china vases made for William and Mary.

Between the King's and Queen's state apartments is the Communication Gallery, which contains pictures of the 'Windsor beauties' — portraits by Sir Peter Lely of some of the noblewomen of Charles II's court.

The ghost of Catherine Howard, Henry VIII's fifth wife, is said to frequent the Haunted Gallery. Before she was sent to the Tower of London, she escaped from her room and ran to where the king was hearing Mass in the Royal Closet. The guards dragged her, screaming, back to her chambers. The most notable feature of the Chapel Royal is the carved and gilded ceiling, which was added by Henry VIII. Many of the later features were added by Wren.

From here, visitors can walk down into the King's beer cellar, wine cellar and great kitchen (still fitted with ovens, spits and utensils). On the eastern side of the Palace there are several gardens of various designs, including a small 'knot garden', laid out in 1924 to show the shape and style of gardens favoured in the sixteenth century.

There are also a Tudor tennis court, maze — which with its six-feet high hedges has intrigued visitors since Queen Anne's day, and the great vine, planted in 1769. The vine has a 7-foot girth at ground level, the main stem is 100 feet long, and it still produces fruit (on sale to visitors in late summer).

Practical details: The State Apartments, Great Kitchens and Cellars, and Tudor Tennis Court are open Monday to Saturday, May to September, from 9.30 am to 6 pm. In March, April and October the closing time is 5 pm, and from November to February it is 4 pm. On Sundays from May to September it is open from 11 am to 6 pm, in October, March and April until 5 pm, and between November and February until 4 pm. There is an admission charge to these areas.

The Gardens (Great Vine, King's Privy Garden, Great Fountain Gardens, Tudor and Elizabethan Knot Gardens, Broad Walk and Wilderness) are open daily until dusk, but not later than 9 pm. Free admission.

The Maze is open Monday to Saturday, May to September, from 10 am to 6 pm. In March, April and October the closing time is 5 pm. On Sundays from May to September it is open from 11 am to 6 pm, and in March, April and October it closes at 5 pm. It is closed from November to February. There is an admission charge. The nearest British Rail station is Hampton Court (SR). Use buses 111, 131, 152, 201, 216 or 267. Easy parking. Open spaces nearby. Refreshments available.

Address: East Molesey, Surrey K78 9AU.

HEALTH AND SAFETY CENTRE

Is your hazard really necessary?

Ways to achieve a safer working day

Every day, two or three people are accidentally killed in British industry, and about 700 are injured. Many of these accidents could have been avoided.

This Centre is administered by the Health and Safety Executive. Its function is to provide information about health and safety problems and the ways in which the Executive has helped to solve them.

The exhibitions here emphasise the basic principles involved in the elimination of risk in occupational hazards. They are designed as groundwork for health and safety training and used by individual business concerns and safety training bodies. Many of the exhibitions include safety appliances currently available.

Lecture demonstrations on industrial hazards are given twice a day by HM Inspectors of Health and Safety. The films produced by the Executive are shown and used as a basis for discussion, and visitors can ask the Inspectors questions about their own particular problems.

Most of the exhibitions are self-explanatory and cover a wide range of subjects, including woodworking machinery, the construction industry,

Special clothing to reduce risk in industry.

ionising radiations, environmental testing and asbestos. To get full advantage of the facilities provided, a full day should be spent at the centre, with either the morning or afternoon 'booked' for the lecture demonstrations and so on.

The centre also provides an information and advisory service which is particularly useful to safety officers, safety representatives, industrial hygienists and others with responsibility for health and safety in the work-place.

Practical details: Open Monday to Friday from 10 am to 4.30 pm. Parties who wish to take part in lecture demonstrations, films and discussions should book well in advance. Free admission. Nearest British Rail station is Victoria (SR). Nearest Underground station is St James's Park. Use buses 10, 11, 24, 29, 88 or 507.

Address: 97 Horseferry Road SW1P 2DY. Telephone (01) 828 9255.

HOGARTH'S HOUSE

Drawn from strife

Savage satirical pictures of the seventeenth-century social scene

Whatever painter and engraver William Hogarth lacked in physical stature — he was only five feet tall — he made up with vigour in his work, attacking relentlessly the twin targets of authority and immorality in eighteenth-century England.

Hogarth, born in 1697, lived in his Chiswick home as a change from his town house in what is now Leicester Square, London. The Chiswick house has survived much, including bombs in the London Blitz of September 1940. After years of dereliction, it is now a museum with scores of examples of Hogarth prints.

Though a great painter, Hogarth disdained traditional themes and preferred to comment on the social scene, often with cynicism and savagery. In pictures shown here he is seen to attack quackery among doctors, excessive drinking and its squalid by-products of poverty and debauchery (*Gin Lane*), British foreign policy *(The Times),* and his own supposed failure in *Finis* or *The Bathos.*

The artist as social commentator emerges in several famous series of pictures, *The Harlot's Progress,* the *Election,* and *Marriage a la Mode* (see the National Gallery, page 97), which are worth close scrutiny as much for their amusing detail as for their general message.

The only colour picture on show is a beautifully sensitive portrait of Mary Lewis, his servant, which makes a pleasing contrast to one of Hogarth's most unpalatable series, *The Four Stages of Cruelty.*

Hogarth himself appears in *Hogarth before the Commandant of Calais.* In the picture he is proving, by virtue of his sketches, that he was bent on nothing more sinister than art when in Calais. It was a close-run thing, though, for Hogarth was told that but for the newly-signed Peace of Aix-la-Chapelle, he would have been hanged. There are the original copper plates for the larger of two sets of illustrations for *Hudibras,* Samuel Butler's satirical poem, and a reproduction of *The Shrimp Girl,* one of his most famous works.

In another series, Hogarth is at his moralistic best. He pursues the respective careers of one diligent and one idle apprentice. Their paths diverge: the former becomes Lord Mayor of London and the latter, tried by him, is condemned to death for murder and hanged at Tyburn.

There is a varied collection of bygones throughout the house: books, receipts, furniture of Hogarth's period, and newspaper cuttings.

Practical details: Open from April to September, on weekdays from 11 am to 6 pm and on Sunday from 2 to 6 pm. From October to March, open on weekdays (not Tuesday) from 11 am to 4 pm and on Sunday from 2 to 4 pm. Parties may visit by arrangement. There is an admission charge. Nearest Underground station is Turnham Green. Use buses E3, 27, 233, 267 or 290.

Address: Hogarth Lane, Chiswick W4 2QN. Telephone (01) 994 6757.

HORNIMAN MUSEUM

Man and his new environment

His clothes, weapons, tools . . . the effects of evolution, and even the instruments he plays

The Horniman Museum, one of the biggest museums outside Central London, was founded by Frederick J Horniman, MP, head of the tea firm. A much-travelled man who collected items of interest wherever he went, Horniman opened his large collection to the public in 1890 at his home in Forest Hill. A few years later, the present building was presented, with the adjoining gardens, to Londoners through the medium of the London County Council.

The exhibits all concern man and his environment. There are displays showing how man in different societies lived and looked after himself — what he wore, the tools he used, the weapons he wielded in hunting or to defend himself.

In the ground floor's South Hall is an ancient Egyptian tomb, found at Abydos around 3000 BC. The skeleton lies in the tomb surrounded, as was customary, by vessels, ornaments and weapons, some of which are broken to signify that the dead man had finished with this world and was prepared for the next.

There are at least a dozen Egyptian mummies of human beings and animals, all excellently preserved, and a large group of figures of gods worshipped in some of the great non-Christian religions, Hinduism, Buddhism and Jainism.

In the Cult of the Dead section, there are mummified bodies — one of a dead chief from New Hebrides, in the west Pacific, whose head contains a skull, but whose body has been grotesquely modelled on a bamboo framework.

On the way up to the aquarium, on the second level, are several other sombre exhibits; centuries-old shackles and other means of restraint for criminals, and an elaborate iron torture chair used in the seventeenth century by the Spanish Inquisition for extracting confessions. The victim, held by manacles, had devices screwed on to his head, and into ears, nose and mouth to inflict pain.

In the aquarium is a glass beehive, and hundreds of live bees can be seen at work on their honeycomb. There is also a large model cross-section of a worker bee. Among the live creatures usually represented are terrapins, mirror carp, eel, lobster, stick insects and silkworms.

In the adjacent North Hall there are hundreds of stuffed birds, including a peacock, eagle and emu, and exhibits comparing different human racial characteristics and the effects of evolution.

Along the North Hall balcony there are impressive displays of crustaceans and fossils. A mid-nineteenth-century Apostle Clock at one end is of exceptional interest: some of the figures in this ornate carved walnut clock have been constructed to enact scenes from the life of Christ on the strike of four o'clock.

The museum has unique collections of musical instruments, past and

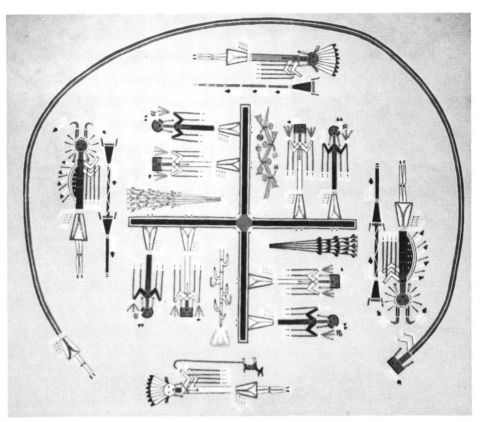

Sandpainting by a Navaho Indian at the Horniman Museum, one of the biggest and most varied museums outside central London.

present, from many parts of the world. Many of them are in the famous Carse Collection. They range from nineteenth-century harps to a Fiji drum hollowed out from a log.

In the modernized West Hall various special exhibitions are staged for periods of about six months. Each has a theme: for example, American Indians.

The museum has an education centre (with three fulltime teachers on the staff) where adults may take courses associated with the museum's interests. Children are given talks, illustrated with films and slides, as a prelude to tours of exhibits. A children's club, with the emphasis on arts and crafts, meets on Saturdays and in school holidays.

Practical details: Open Monday to Saturday from 10.30 am to 6 pm, and on Sunday from 2 to 6 pm. Free admission. Nearest British Rail station is Forest Hill (SR). Use buses 12, 12A, 63, 122, 171, 185 or 194. Open spaces nearby. Refreshments available.

Address: London Road, Forest Hill SE23 3PQ. Telephone (01) 699 2339 and (01) 699 1872.

The beginning of television

What an early studio looked like . . . how a series is made

The world's first regular television broadcast was made in Britain on 2nd November 1936. It was the climax of years of experiment, and the Gallery of the Independent Broadcasting Authority tells the enthralling story from the beginning, with the aid of instruments actually made by the pioneers, or replicas.

Television began with photography, and photography began in the mid-1800s with the Daguerreotype — a form of 'still' photograph using sunlight and named after Louis Daguerre. In 1867 came the Zoetrope, or 'wheel of life', and in 1895 the Mutoscope, which with its 700 figures ranged round a drum gave the impression of animation when flicked rapidly, the principle employed in the movie film.

Ten years later came the Bioscope, a gas-lit, hand-powered cine projector. Meanwhile, Sir William Crookes had been experimenting with a cathode ray tube in the 1870s, and, as is demonstrated in the Gallery, succeeded in creating the image of a Maltese Cross.

In 1908, Campbell Swinton wrote to

A replica of the TV camera, which John Logie Baird first demonstrated in 1926.

Nature magazine, outlining the principle of 'distant electric vision', thus becoming known as the father of modern television.

In the 1920s two methods of transmitting the image were being developed — the 'mechanical' system of John Logie Baird, and an electronic system which had been produced by Marconi and EMI. The Government asked the BBC to try out both in their transmissions of 1936, and eventually chose the electronic method.

The gallery gives a practical demonstration of how a television image is made up — of one spot of light flashing along the 625 lines of the television screen at 12,000 mph, giving the illusion of a moving picture — in fact 25 slightly different 'still' pictures a second.

One of the interesting features here is a reproduction of the BBC's television transmission studio at Alexandra Palace as it was in 1936, complete with lamps, one camera, a microphone boom, and a floor covered with snaking electric cables — all made to one-third actual size. The visitor can see illustrations of the kind of

programmes put out then, and the improved ones which benefited from new techniques after World War II, when transmissions resumed. Independent television came along in 1955, and an exhibit shows, using illuminated photographs, models and actual costumes, how the television series *Frontier* was written and produced. This includes a sound recording of a discussion between producer and script editor, the scripts themselves, models of the set used in production and, finally, film extracts from the finished programme.

The tour of the gallery concludes with a short description by the guide on the functions of the Independent Broadcasting Authority in maintaining high standards of television programmes and advertising, by 'vetting' them before transmission (20 per cent of advertisements are rejected), and giving advice to the regional programme companies who are under contract to them and hire the IBA's transmitters.

The visitor is also introduced to Independent Television News, with a talk enlivened by behind-the-scenes pictures of its work on *News at Ten*. A vivid display explains how colour television works and what it involves in the studio, and there is the story of radio and a description of the new Independent Local Radio service.

Practical details: Visits, in the form of conducted tours, may be made by prior arrangement during normal office hours. Free admission. Nearest Underground station is Knightsbridge. Use buses 14, 19, 22, 30, 52, 73, 74 or 137.

Address: 70 Brompton Road SW3 1EY. Telephone: (01) 584 7011.

IMPERIAL WAR MUSEUM

In defence of the Realm

Mighty battleship guns, fighting aircraft, the first tanks, and V1 and V2 rockets . . . The machinery of war gives silent warning

After World War II, Field Marshal Viscount Montgomery and the War Office were engaged in a small battle of their own. The Field Marshal claimed that the motorised campaign caravans that he used as his headquarters in the field belonged to him, and the War Office considered them as the property of the nation. Peace terms were agreed: Monty could keep the caravans during his lifetime; thereafter they would be returned to the nation.

In fact, the three caravans, restored and containing lifesize figures of Monty and other officers, have a gallery to themselves in the Imperial War Museum, and while visitors inspect them, the tape-recorded voice of Monty, explaining their background, can be heard.

The Map caravan was his tactical HQ until 1945, and it was to this that the Germans came to discuss surrender

Massive 15-inch naval guns greet the visitor to the Imperial War Museum.

terms on Luneberg Heath in Germany. The Mack caravan, which had been used by Rommel, the German desert army leader, was captured from the Italians in North Africa. 'I would turn out of it for only two people,' said Monty. 'The King (George VI) and Winston Churchill.' Nearby are Monty's black double-badged beret and battledress, one of the famous British 25-pounder guns, and a tableau representing army life, with tank, carrier and troops, in North-West Europe.

In the armoured vehicles section is a Matilda tank, one of a breed which achieved fame in North Africa. Also on this floor are early tanks and guns from World War I.

Also here are field guns, the 13-pounder from which the first shot on land was fired in World War I, and several howitzers, British and German. The two biggest guns in the museum stand imposingly in the large grassed forecourt. These are the last two surviving 15-inch British naval guns, relics of battleships *Ramillies* and *Resolution*. Each weighs about 100 tons, and had a range of about 16 miles.

A trench warfare section describes how World War I troops lived, the kind of uniforms they wore, their equipment and their rations. There is also a display on the causes of World War I, a feature on the development of warships, and a number of ship models.

The air weapons section offers a chance to see many historic aircraft, including the BE2c, Bristol F2B and Camel from World War I, and a Mark I Spitfire, Mosquito, Focke Wulf 190 (the Germans' crack fighter) and Heinkel HE162 from World War II.

The front section of a Lancaster heavy bomber, which actually went on operations, can be seen at close quarters.

Hitler's rocket weapons against London and the south-east, the V1 and V2, are both on show. The V2 is partly cut away to show the engine and warhead.

Models include a special exhibit on the Dambusters' raid, with photographs and maps showing how it was planned.

A small permanent exhibition is given over to the Victoria Cross and George Cross. Here are uniforms and the actual medals won by several heroes of both world wars.

The records of Group Captain Leonard Cheshire are displayed, along with his flying kit. Cheshire's award was practically unique: he won the Victoria Cross not for a single heroic act but for four years of courage and leadership in Bomber Command. The role of Resistance agents is also acknowledged, with George Cross exhibits of agents Wing Commander F Yeo-Thomas (The White Rabbit) and Violette Szabo, who was killed after torture.

Visitors can see the wartime uniforms of several leaders, including King George V, Field-Marshal Lord Haig (both from World War I), and Admiral of the Fleet Lord Mountbatten, Field-Marshal Lord Alexander and Marshal of the RAF Lord Douglas (all from World War II).

A special exhibit marks the noble part in the Battle of Britain played by nearly 3,000 of the 'Few'.

Two rooms contain displays associated with the Mountbatten family ('A Century of Service') and the late Duke of Gloucester ('Soldier

Royal'). These contain uniforms, decorations, orders, scrolls and mementoes, and form small but colourful tributes to two noble names. Several historic documents can be seen in the museum, including the German Instrument of Surrender in the World War II, signed by Field Marshal Montgomery and the German military leaders. There is the controversial Anglo-German Agreement, a non-aggression 'pact' signed at Munich by the British Prime Minister, Neville Chamberlain, and Adolf Hitler in 1938. Also, Hitler's 'political testament', which he dictated shortly before committing suicide and signed together with Martin Bormann and Dr Goebbels. A new art gallery displays a wide range of pictures from both world wars.

Selections from the collection of 9,000 pictures in the museum's possession are frequently shown in special temporary exhibitions. Application to see the reserve collection may be made to the Keeper of the Art Department. Public film shows are normally given throughout the week, except Mondays. Programmes of activities for schools, including talks and films, are arranged during term time. Applications should be made to the Schools Officer.

Practical details: Open Monday to Saturday from 10 am to 6 pm, and on Sunday from 2 to 6 pm. Free admission. Nearest British Rail station is Waterloo (SR). Nearby Underground stations are Lambeth North and Elephant & Castle. Use buses 3, 10, 12, 44, 45, 53, 63, 68, 184 or 188. Open spaces nearby. Refreshments available.
Address: Lambeth Road SE1 6HZ. Telephone (01) 735 8922.

JEWISH MUSEUM

A store of Jewish treasures

An Ark from sixteenth-century Venice; propaganda 'money' from Nazi concentration camps . . .

Housed in the same building as the office of the Chief Rabbi, this museum is a delight to the eye; yet though it was opened as long ago as 1932, many Jews are unaware of its existence. Though comparatively small, it is crowded with treasures, ritual objects and mementoes. The oddest, perhaps the oldest and certainly the biggest of these is a ten-foot-high synagogue Ark from sixteenth-century Venice. It is made of Italian walnut, carved, coloured and gilded. Above the arch is the Hebrew text *Know before Whom thou standest,* and its doors open to reveal bells and Scrolls of the Law (the five books of Moses).

There are some exquisite examples of silver work among the pointers, spice boxes, rimmonim (bells) and Chanukah menorahs (candlesticks) of the seventeenth and eighteenth centuries, and some Passover dishes in majolica ware, as well as silver, china and pewter. One Chanukah candlestick, in jewelled silver filigree, was made in 1558; another example is collapsible for travelling.

There are many cases for Scrolls of Esther used at Purim, which are decorated with silver work.

There is one sombre note. Of the

murder of six million Jews by the Nazis in World War II, there are only token exhibits in the museum: concentration camp paper money printed by the Germans at Theresienstadt, in Czechoslovakia, in the fraudulent hope that it would be regarded as a model ghetto. The other exhibit is a Star of David badge worn in the camp.

Practical details: Open Monday to Thursday from 2.30 to 5 pm, and on Friday and Sunday from 10.30 am to 12.45 pm. Closed on national and Jewish holidays. Free admission. Nearest British Rail station is Euston (LMR), and nearest Underground station is Euston Square. Use Buses 14, 18, 30, 68, 73 or 77.

Address: Woburn House, Upper Woburn Place WC1H 0EP. Telephone (01) 387 3081.

KEATS HOUSE

Poet's corner

Here Keats found the love of his life and wrote 'To a Nightingale'

There is a plum tree in the garden of Wentworth Place, the delightful white-painted home of John Keats: it is a successor of the original tree beneath which he wrote the memorable lines of the ode 'To a Nightingale' one May morning in 1819.

Keats lived at Wentworth Place, which was really two semi-detached houses, for a little less than two highly productive years. He occupied two rooms of the building and once lived next door to Fanny Brawne. They were very much in love and became engaged in 1819. She and her mother nursed Keats for a time towards the end of his short life: he died when he was only 25.

In the Brawne Rooms there is a Hepplewhite dining-table which belonged to Leigh Hunt, the writer and essayist who gave Keats so much encouragement. And in a glass case a selection of mementoes — Fanny's lorgnettes, locks of her hair, purses, needlecases and her engagement ring from Keats. There is also a marble bust of the poet.

Keats's sitting-room is unchanged. It was here that his friend Charles Brown found the manuscript of 'To a Nightingale' hidden behind books in

The Venetian Ark, at the Jewish Museum, is thought to have been made for Jews who had fled the Inquisition.

a cupboard.

Keats's writing desk is in the Chester Room, and in glass cases are many of his letters, first editions of his works, and his own books.

There is a touching letter from Keats to Mrs Brawne, mother of Fanny, sent from Naples harbour on the 24th October 1820:

'I dare not fix my Mind upon Fanny, I have not dared to think of her. The only comfort I have had that way has been in thinking for hours together of having the knife she gave me put in a silver case — the hair in a Locket — and the Pocket Book in a gold net. Show her this. I dare say no more — Yet [you] must not believe I am so ill as this Letter may look . . . Goodbye Fanny! god bless you.'

It was the last letter he ever sent the Brawnes before his death in Rome from 'consumption' in 1821.

Keats House, which was built in 1815, was in danger of destruction in 1920-21 but was saved by public subscription, largely from the USA. Camden Borough Council had it restored and refurbished in 1974-75. Gifts of relics have been donated by descendants of Fanny Brawne, Fanny Keats, Leigh Hunt, and Keats's other friends, Charles Wentworth Dilke and Charles Armitage Brown.

Practical details: Open Monday to Saturday from 10 am to 6 pm, and on Sunday from 2 to 5 pm. Party tours may be made by arrangement. Free admission. Nearest British Rail station is Hampstead Heath (LMR). Nearby Underground stations are Hampstead and Belsize Park. Use buses C11, 24, 46 or 268.

Address: Wentworth Place, Keats Grove, Hampstead NW3 2RR. Telephone (01) 435 2062.

KENSINGTON PALACE (STATE APARTMENTS)

Birthplace of queens

A favourite royal residence during several reigns, set in spacious public gardens

Kensington Palace, which contains much architectural work by Sir Christopher Wren, was the main London residence of the late Stuart and early Hanoverian monarchs until George II's time. It is still the home of several members of the Royal Family, including Princess Margaret, Princess Alice Countess of Athlone, the Kents and Gloucesters, who live in the private wings. The State Apartments, however, are open to the public.

The first reminder of the Palace's royal connections is on the Broad Walk approach to it in the park — a statue of Queen Victoria in 1837. It was sculpted by her daughter Princess Louise for the residents of Kensington to mark her Golden Jubilee in 1887. Queen Victoria was born here and so was Queen Mary, wife of King George V. Kensington Palace was the official centre of the court in William and Mary's time.

Visitors first go up the oaken Queen's Staircase into Queen Mary's Gallery, hung with many portraits, including a fine one of Peter the Great in armour, painted by Sir Godfrey Kneller when the Czar was visiting London in 1698, and another of William III and Queen Mary by Willem Wissing.

Along the Queen's side of the palace, one passes through the closet, dining-room (which still has its original panelling), drawing room, bedchamber, and so to the privy chamber. The ceiling here was painted by William Kent for George I and shows Mars and Minerva, with Mars wearing the Order of the Garter and Minerva attended by the arts and sciences. There is more ceiling painting by Kent in the Presence Chamber, notable because its arabesque decoration in the Pompeian style was making its first appearance in English decorative painting.

Kent made a large and intriguing painting on the King's Grand Staircase — in the 'illusionist' style.

The whole wall gives the impression of people crowding arched balconies overlooking the staircase. The entire design is on canvas stretched out and fixed to the wall.

In the King's Gallery, where William III was taken ill in 1702, shortly after a riding accident at Hampton Court, are mythological ceiling pictures by Kent, and a number of seventeenth-century Flemish, Italian and Spanish pictures, the most important being *Jupiter and Antiope* by Rubens and Van Dyck's fine *Cupid and Psyche*.

The rooms used by Queen Victoria as a child have recently been decorated and hung with pictures from the early Victorian period, so as to give an impression of the times when she lived there with her mother. In the Ante-room there is a glass case showing her Georgian-style doll's house and some of her toys. The small wax doll wearing a crown was given to her eldest daughter in 1850. In Queen Victoria's bedroom, the new young queen first heard of her accession in 1837. In this room Queen Mary was born in 1867.

The lavishly-decorated Cupola Room was once the main state room of the palace, with a fine ceiling, wall columns and gilded statuary. Here, the baby Victoria was baptised in 1819, and beneath is the Red Saloon where she held her first Privy Council on the morning of her accession to the throne.

Near the Palace is the Orangery, designed by Nicholas Hawksmoor and Vanbrugh for Queen Anne and built in 1704. The interior is impressive, with white-painted panelled walls, classical statues and columns, and arches with fine carvings by Grinling Gibbons.

Do not forget to peep through the foliage at the Sunken Garden, with its fountains playing and its colourful all-the-year display of flowers. The garden was laid out in Edwardian times, but it is a reminder of the formal gardens that were in vogue at Kensington before the eighteenth century.

Practical details: Open March to September, Monday to Saturday from 10 am to 6 pm and on Sunday from 2 to 6 pm. Also open during the winter months, but closing at 5 pm in October and February each day, and at 4 pm in November, December and January. There is an admission charge. Nearby Underground stations are Queensway, Bayswater and High Street Kensington. Use buses 9, 12, 27, 28, 31, 33, 49, 52, 73 or 88. Set in open spaces.

Address: Kensington Gardens, off High Street, Kensington W8.

KENWOOD HOUSE

Woodland haven in Hampstead

Famous works of art in a magnificent mansion . . . and concerts across the lake

Kenwood House's history began with John Bill, the King's Printer, who is thought to have had the original house built soon after 1616. The present building is the second one, which was remodelled in classical style for Lord Mansfield, Lord Chief Justice, 1964-78, by the distinguished Scottish architect Robert Adam.
In 1925 the Earl of Iveagh saved the house from demolition by buying it and, two years later, he left Kenwood to the nation.
One of the results of Robert Adam's work was the fine north front portico, with its four fluted columns. Another is the magnificent library, or Adam Room, which with its gilded mouldings and Zucchi ceiling paintings must be one of the noblest examples of Adam's interior design. Kenwood contains many distinguished paintings, the best known of which are Rembrandt's *Portrait of the Artist* (perhaps the most extraordinary of the artist's sixty self-portraits), and Vermeer's *The Guitar Player*. The latter vanished in 1974 after being stolen one night by intruders. It was found, undamaged, in a churchyard soon afterwards. There are paintings by Sir Joshua Reynolds, Thomas Gainsborough, Frans Hals, Boucher, Van Dyck,

Romney, Stubbs (his painting of the horse Whistlejacket is on long-term loan from Earl Fitzwilliam), and Landseer. There is one early picture by J M W Turner, *Fishermen on a Lee Shore,* which makes an interesting contrast with his later work.
The 74 acres of parkland — mainly beeches, oaks and chestnuts — around Kenwood are also open to the public. In the summer, concerts are given in an enclosure on the south side, the orchestra performing from an acoustic shell on the far side of the lake. Chamber music and poetry recitals take place in the Orangery on Sundays in spring and autumn. The whole setting, on a warm evening, is pure delight to ear and eye.
Practical details: Open daily. From April to September from 10 am to 7 pm, in October, February and March from 10 am to 5 pm, and between November and January from 10 am to 4 pm. Free admission. Use bus 210 from Golders Green or Archway Underground station; or from Hampstead Underground station use bus 268 to Whitestone Pond then change to bus 210. Easy parking. Set in open space. Refreshments available.
Address: Hampstead Lane NW3 7JR. Telephone (01) 348 1286.

KEW BRIDGE ENGINES MUSEUM

Dinosaurs of the steam age

Here some of the biggest and oldest engines in the world can be seen in action

Every weekend they get really steamed up about things down Kew Bridge way. And they have plenty to get steamed up about — several massive ancient pump engines, housed in a water supply pumping station. They are a marvel of Victorian expertise. 'Dinosaurs of the steam age' someone has called them — it was machines like these that launched Britain as an industrial nation.

First, an 1898 steam-hammer can be seen at work in the forge, where running repairs to the old pump engines used to be carried out. Today, there is a blacksmith at work. The neighbouring machine shop, with its array of belt-driven machinery, produced any parts required (there were no instantly available 'spares' then). The 192-feet-tall Stand Pipe Tower nearby contains vertical pipes into which the great engines pumped water; this was partly as a safeguard against mains failure, but also to maintain constant pressure in local mains.

In the old West Engine House stands a huge Boulton & Watt beam engine, which came into use in 1820 — five years before Stephenson's 'Rocket'. This is the second oldest working engine in the world, and is modelled

The largest beam engine under steam in the world.

on the old Cornish-type engines used to pump water out of the Cornish tin and copper mines. With these engines, there is not a smooth continuous whirr as with the modern type. There is a gradual build-up of power ... then a huge thrust, or rather leap, as the piston descends in the 64-inch-diameter cylinder below one end of the overhead beam — high in the roof — and the heavily weighted plunger rises into the pump barrel below the other end. It is a sight not to be missed or forgotten, especially as the whole cycle can be seen at close quarters. Visitors can climb up into the roof and watch the great 15-ton cast-iron beam rock impressively on its pivot.

Other engines on show include one built in 1838, which worked until 1944 principally supplying Ealing with water. Also the now-unique Bull engine, which has no beam because the steam cylinder is directly over the pump.

In the old boiler house is a different kind of engine, a 'compound rotative', which has a flywheel 18 feet in diameter, and a crank-shaft. It was built in 1863. There are two horizontal steam engines of a different type, and also a variety of small model steam engines, all busily in action.

The climax of one's visit comes with watching one of the two largest engines on show, in the '90'- and '100'-inch Engine House. Both beam engines, the first has a cylinder diameter of 90 inches, a beam weighing 35 tons, and pumps up 472 gallons of water at a single stroke. It is the largest beam engine under steam in the world, and seems to know it!

Sadly, its 100-inch companion, with an awesome beam weighing around 50 tons and capable of pumping 717 gallons at one massive stroke of its pump, is at present out of action.

Practical details: Open on Saturday and Sunday from 11 am to 5 pm. Also open on Bank Holiday Monday. There is an admission charge. Nearest British Rail station is Kew Bridge (SR) and nearest Underground station is Gunnersbury. Use buses 15 (Sunday only), 27, 65, 237 or 267. Easy parking. Refreshments available.

Address: Kew Bridge Road, Brentford, Middlesex. Telephone (01) 568 4757.

KINGSBURY WATER MILL MUSEUM

A working water mill

A restored mill that was in use until the 1960s

Most museums are still and quiet, but the visitor walks round this one to the accompaniment of rushing waters, and the waterwheel keeps turning in the River Ver below.

The building's date is uncertain, but it is believed to be Elizabethan (that great Elizabethan, Sir Francis Bacon, lived at Gorhambury nearby). Two hundred years ago, in Georgian times, a brick front was added, and since then the mill has been unchanged.

The mill has three grinding stones, and all are driven by the waterwheel. This mill was used to grind corn right up until the 1960s, but then it fell into disuse. It was restored in 1970 and is now in full working order — one of the few buildings listed as ancient monuments that are still in action. Some of the miller's tools, such as chisels for 'dressing' the millstones with furrows, can be seen; also gin traps and farm implements.

Practical details: Open daily from 10 am to 5 pm, all year round. There is an admission charge, though special rates are available for party bookings. Nearest British Rail station is St Albans City (LMR). Use buses 84, 320, 330, or Green Line coaches 724 or 727. Easy parking.

Address: St Michael's Street, St Albans, Hertfordshire. Telephone St Albans 53323.

KODAK MUSEUM

A hundred and fifty years of photography

A copy of the earliest surviving photograph and a host of historic cameras

It is a long and fascinating journey from man's early attempts to make a pictorial record of the world about him with a simple 'camera obscura' to the complex, highly sophisticated camera of today.

This museum, with more than 6,000 items of equipment and thousands of photographs to draw upon, brings the story into sharp focus, while paying proper tribute to Kodak's own important role in popularizing an interest which until the 1880s was enjoyed only by a few.

Among the early exhibits is a late eighteenth-century camera obscura, and a copy of the earliest surviving photograph — of a view from a window overlooking a courtyard in Chalon-sur-Saône, taken by J N Niepce in 1826. The exposure time was eight hours.

Examples of Fox Talbot's Calotype work, and a replica of his 'mousetrap' camera of 1835 keep company with his *Pencil of Nature,* the first book to be published with photographs.

Other exhibits include an example of the first camera to be sold to the public — the Daguerreotype, signed by Daguerre. Also a large wooden camera, sold by Giroux; and one of the few surviving original all-metal cameras made by Voigtlander in 1841. After various improvements in film had been made, Dr R L Maddox devised a system for taking snapshots, using his gelatin dry-plate process, and hand-held cameras were introduced. There are a number of interesting original cameras which exploited the roll film, thereby dispensing with the plate: the No 1 Kodak, designed by George Eastman, founder of Kodak Ltd. in 1888, sold loaded with a roll film for 100 exposures. Total price: £5 5s.

It was the roll film which opened up the field of photography. Kodak's slogan was 'You press the button, we do the rest'. Not only a convenience, but also good business. No longer did the photographer have to develop and print pictures; this could be done for him if he chose.

In the late nineteenth century, photography was already becoming an art, and the work of three specialists in pictorial camera work, Frank M Sutcliffe, George Davison and Paul Martin is liberally acknowledged with examples of their skill.

In 1925, the Leica camera began a trend towards 35 mm film cameras, which are now in vogue. Cameras demonstrating developments through the years, are on show — from Kodak's popular Brownies of the early 1900s to today's Instamatic camera.

There are several strange relics from the field of photography. In the latter part of the last century, there were a number of 'detective' cameras in use, and several are displayed. One example is the circular camera by C P Stirn of Berlin, which hung round the neck, while the lens poked through a waistcoat buttonhole. Another exhibit ·

As we were: a Victorian photographer.

from this period is a special chair for photographing criminals, used in Paris in the 1880s. Its uncomfortable fitments forced the criminal to sit square — and still.

Practical details: Open Monday to Friday from 9.30 am to 4.30 pm, by appointment only. Free admission. Nearest British Rail *and* Underground station is Harrow & Wealdstone. Use buses 114, 182, 186, 258, 286 or H1. Easy parking.

Address: Kodak Ltd, Headstone Drive, Wealdstone, Harrow, Middlesex HA1 4TY. Telephone (01) 427 4380, extension 76.

NOTE: This information is accurate at the time of writing, but the museum is due to have new premises built, the date for which is uncertain.

LANCASTER HOUSE

Home of the Grand Old Duke of York

A building of great splendour where the Government plays host to distinguished foreign guests

Sir Winston Churchill gave a banquet in Lancaster House for Queen Elizabeth II a few days after her Coronation in 1953. This is the best surviving example of early Victorian architecture and is the centre of

Government hospitality as well as having been the setting for several important international and Commonwealth conferences.

Lancaster House was built by the (Grand Old) Duke of York to the design of Benjamin Wyatt, who altered Apsley House (see Wellington Museum, page 153), at Hyde Park Corner. The interior has a French-style decor of great splendour, with fluted columns, crystal chandeliers, wall paintings and gilded and coloured ceilings.

The Staircase Hall, which was decorated by Sir Charles Barry, is suitably grand — certainly the most imposing feature of the building and soaring to its full height. Again, the ceiling is beautifully patterned. The staircase balustrade is in gold and white rococo style, with torcheres, originally fed by oil, flanking the foot of the stairs.

Sir Winston's Coronation Banquet was held in the Great Gallery, on the first floor, so-called because of its immense length — 120 feet. In the Music Room, used as a state dining-room in the days of the Dukes of Sutherland (owners after the Duke of York), Chopin is supposed to have played before Queen Victoria.

Practical details: Open from Easter to mid-December on Saturday and Sunday from 2 to 6 pm. Also open on Easter Monday and Spring and Summer Bank Holidays at the same time. There is an admission charge. Nearest Underground station is Green Park. Use buses 14, 19, 22 or 38. **Address:** Stable Yard, St James's SW1A 1BB.

The imposing Grand Staircase at Lancaster House.

High Victorian art

Exotic rooms in the home of a former President of the Royal Academy

This house was built during Lord Leighton's presidency of the Royal Academy (1878 to 1896) to meet his individual taste and needs as an artist; a happy piece of co-operation between him and the architect, his friend George Aitchison, RA.

The house, owned by Kensington and Chelsea Borough Council, is now a gallery of high Victorian art. It has a number of unique features, the most exotic of which is the Arab Hall, an authentic reconstruction by Aitchison based on drawings which he made in Moorish Spain.

The hall incorporates some particularly fine tiling of the thirteenth, fifteenth and seventeenth centuries, which Leighton collected with Sir Richard Burton, the explorer, from Rhodes, Damascus and Cairo. The small pool and its single-jet fountain were sculpted from a single black marble block. There is a Persian-style mosaic frieze in brown, blue, silver and gold by Walter Crane. Marble columns, with capitals carved by Sir Edgar Boehm, Queen's Sculptor, and Richard Caldicot, support a dome, and there are stained-glass windows.

Rich deep blue tiles by William De Morgan, sometimes inset with a fifteenth-century tile, decorate the hall

The Arab Hall, Leighton House, authentically reconstructed by Aitchison, based on drawings from Moorish Spain.

and staircase. It is dominated by a copy of Michelangelo's *Creation of Adam* in the Sistine Chapel, done by Leighton while still a student of 19. In the gallery at the head of the staircase are Ford Madox Brown's *Head of a Girl* and two paintings by Burne-Jones for his Holy Grail series. Works in oils and water-colours, and drawings which are mainly studies for major works by Leighton, are displayed in the house's only bedroom.

Lord Leighton was a considerable painter, now being increasingly admired, and a superlative draughtsman, which the host of paintings and drawings on show make clear. His great studio is used today as a concert hall and recital room. But it still contains the dais under the window where his models would recline, later to withdraw discreetly through a small door opposite leading downstairs.

There are a number of interesting pictures here, among them *Hearts are Trumps,* a canvas by Millais; *Christ Lamenting over Jerusalem* by Sir Charles Eastlake PRA; *For He Had Great Possessions* by G F Watts; *Rehearsing the Service* by Alphonse Le Gross; *Miss Alexander* by Whistler; and a large study in oils for *Clytie* by Leighton, whose *Death of Brunelleschi* was painted at the age of 20.

There are also a section of a Watts mural painting, *Study for Chaos* and Burne-Jones's *Morning of the Resurrection.*

The Winter Studio and Perrin Gallery contain numerous pencil studies by Leighton for major works, which would be an admirable object lesson for any art student. *Elisha Raising the Son of the Shunamite* by Leighton is in the Music Room, also *Brunhylda* by G F Watts.

The room also contains a case displaying De Morgan ware. Other cases of De Morgan and post-De Morgan ware may be seen in the house.

Temporary exhibitions of art in all periods and styles, including work by contemporary artists, are held from time to time.

Practical details: Open Monday to Saturday from 11 am to 5 pm. During periods of temporary exhibitions the closing time is 6 pm from Monday to Friday. The garden is open from April to September. Free admission. Nearest Underground station is High Street Kensington. Use buses 9, 9A, 27, 28, 33, 49 or 73.

Address: 12 Holland Park Road W14 8LZ. Telephone (01) 602 3316.

THE LONDON DUNGEON

History's horrors

Torture and execution were once commonplace. They had unpleasant ways of making us talk — or keeping us quiet

A few years ago, a London mother took her children to see the Tower of London, only to have them complain afterwards, in some disappointment: 'But Mum, there was no blood!'

The London Dungeon is the remedy of the mother, Mrs Annabel Geddes, for any similar sense of deprivation among London's young — or old. In 1975, hard by the busy London Bridge railway station, she mounted the goriest permanent show in London, depicting the murkier side of British history in all the horror which attends man's inhumanity to man.

It is a demonstration, too, of a painstaking concern for accuracy and authenticity, reinforced by informative captioning to put the grisly tableaux into their real-life historical context.

Although there are displays featuring Dracula and witchcraft, most of the Dungeon's lifesize scenes, using wax figures, add substance to events which, though mentioned in school text-books, would be highly unlikely to reach the television screen without severe editing: torture and execution in an alarmingly wide variety.

One of the most vivid scenes is a family

The London Dungeon: one of the goriest of the museums, with its grim displays of torture and executions.

suffering a kind of torture inflicted by nature — the Great Plague. And there are live (but harmless) rats of the type which were plague carriers.

The damp-walled railway arches in which the exhibition is housed, lit by eerie green lighting against a dark background, is an appropriately sombre setting for scenes from the Tower of London (one only has to imagine the poor victim's screams from the rack — all the rest is before you).

Although torture never had official sanction in England, it was nevertheless widely practised.

The rack was a common and precisely adjustable mechanism, but others are shown here: 'Little Ease', a stone recess which was too cramped to allow a prisoner to stand, sit or lie down; the pillory; stocks (pretty tame, compared with most others); crushing with heavy stones; branding; and hanging, drawing and quartering.

You can see the martyred bishops Latimer and Ridley being burned at the stake; St George being crucified (just one of his many ordeals); Anne Boleyn being beheaded by a French swordsman; the murder of Thomas a Becket in Canterbury Cathedral; and the executions of Lord Lovat and Charles I.

Practical details: Open daily (including Sunday): April to September from 10 am to 6 pm, and October to March from 10 am to 4.30 pm. There is an admission charge, which is reduced for parties, children and pensioners. Nearest British Rail *and* Underground station is London Bridge (SR). Use buses 10, 35, 40, 44, 47, 48 or 133. Refreshments available. **Address:** 28-34 Tooley Street, SE1 2SZ. Telephone (01) 403 0606.

LONDON PLANETARIUM

Exploring the Universe

The constellations and the planets explained

Here, next door to Madame Tussaud's (see page 84) you can see the heavens, the moon and the myriad stars and planets above the London skyline — all under one roof. All are projected on to the ceiling of a dome by a huge and ingeniously versatile £100,000 Zeiss projector.

Different programmes and lectures are offered. For example; superstitions and the stars; the constellations seen by man from Earth; what you would see from points far out in space, or from other places on the Earth's surface such as Africa or Australia (the

*Above: The Zeiss projector at the
London Planetarium, which projects
the stars onto the ceiling of the dome.
Left: The Planetarium, next to
Madame Tussaud's, is one of
London's most popular tourist
attractions.*

projector can 'take' you there). Special
instructive programmes are arranged
for schools.

Practical details: Performances are
given regularly from 11 am to 5 pm
daily, including Sunday. Telephone
for details of times and admission
charges (on which there is a reduction
for parties). Nearest Underground
station is Baker Street. Use buses 2, 13,
18, 27, 30, 74, 159 or 176.
Refreshments available.

Address: Marylebone Road NW1 5LR.
Telephone (01) 486 1121.

MADAME TUSSAUD'S

The famous and the infamous

All human life is here — in wax: king and commoner, famous and notorious, saintly and evil

Anyone could be looking over your shoulder at Madame Tussaud's . . . William Shakespeare, Sir Winston Churchill, the first men on the moon, or even the Queen. The host of lifelike wax figures which leap from the pages of history and crowd Madame Tussaud's also includes one of the founder herself. Madame Tussaud died in 1850, and her effigy, made at the age of 81, can be seen near the entrance to the Great Hall.

Hers is not the oldest: that honour goes to the waxen likeness of Madame du Barry which, presented as the Sleeping Beauty, can be seen to 'breathe'. It was modelled by Madame Tussaud's uncle in 1765. Two other figures made in the eighteenth century are those of Louis XVI and Marie Antoinette, who were executed during the French Revolution in 1793.

The visitor steps first into the tableaux. Among them are the execution of Mary, Queen of Scots; the Sleeping Beauty figure; and one based on Yeames's famous picture of the Civil War scene, 'When did you last see your father?'. Then the Conservatory, and next 'Heroes' — figures in the worlds of exploration, entertainment and sport, like Muhammad Ali, Marilyn Monroe and

Elton John, with a backing of recorded sound.

In the Grand Hall, time and wax play tricks with a quite disconcerting realism: Queen Elizabeth I, and Henry VIII with his six wives, all standing together; the bellicose Henry V, resplendent in shining armour; Field Marshal Montgomery, anachronistic among the other great generals of history – The Black Prince, Cromwell, Wellington. Also there are the leaders of the Government, the heads of African states, General Booth, founder of the Salvation Army, and the great figures of literature and the arts such as Shakespeare, Henry Moore, and Picasso.

Left: Pablo Picasso, sitting casually in the Grand Hall.
Above: Stark realism at the Battle of Trafalgar.
Right: The Chamber of Horrors.

Many of the figures wear clothes that are realistic representations of ones they wore at some time; and in some cases — including that of Henry Moore — the subject has gone to the trouble of presenting every item of an outfit to the museum to ensure authenticity.

The realism is stark and chilling in the Chamber of Horrors, with its sinister parade of murderers and assassins. Among the grisly relics here are the actual knife blade of the guillotine, which was traced in 1846 by Madame

Tussaud's sons to the grandson of the Paris executioner. There is also a 'lifesize' working model of the guillotine, complete with simulated bloodstains. Nearby are the death masks of Louis XVI, Marie Antoinette and the revolutionary leader Robespierre, which Madame Tussaud was compelled to take immediately after their executions.

Other real-life exhibits include the actual door of the condemned cell at Newgate Prison and the bell that tolled when prisoners left for execution. There is a scaffold from Hertford Gaol dated 1878, which bears a sombre tableau showing the last moments of Charlie Peace, a burglar, with his executioner, Marwood.

The biggest exhibit is a reproduction of the lower gun-deck of the *Victory* at the Battle of Trafalgar, where 40 men can be seen charging and firing four guns, to the accompaniment of flashes, explosions, smoke and the clamour of battle from the deck above. Farther on is the orlop deck, and a poignant scene showing Nelson dying at the moment he receives news of victory. Every effort has been made in this impressive tableau — and, indeed, throughout the museum — to achieve complete accuracy.

Practical details: Open daily, including Sunday, from 10 am. Between April and September it closes at 6 pm, and between October and March at 5.30 pm. Telephone for details of admission charges (on which there is a reduction for parties). Nearest Underground is Baker Street. Use buses 2, 13, 18, 27, 30, 74, 159 or 176.
Refreshments available.
Address: Marylebone Road NW1 5LR. Telephone (01) 935 6861.

MARBLE HILL HOUSE

Snatched from destruction

A villa that the public rescued from demolition . . . where a poet helped to design the gardens

In 66 acres of public parkland stands Marble Hill House, a trim English villa in the style of Palladio. It was built between 1724 and 1729 by Roger Morris for Henrietta Howard, mistress of George II and later Countess of Suffolk. The poet Alexander Pope, who lived near by, was among those who contributed ideas for laying out the grounds.

In 1965 the house came under the wing of the reconstituted Greater London Council, and it was restored to its

original appearance.

Marble Hill House has gradually been fitted out with furniture and paintings to match its style and age. There are excellent examples of carving in walnut and giltwood, and a number of paintings by Reynolds, Wilson, Sir James Thornhill, Gravelot, Mercier, Vanderbank and Phillips. Temporary exhibitions are sometimes held on the ground floor.

Practical details: Open daily, except Friday, from 10 am to 5 pm, but closing at 4 pm between November and January. Free admission. Nearest British Rail station is St Margaret's (SR) and the nearest Underground station is Richmond. Use buses 27, 33, 37, 73, 90, 90B, 202 or 270. Easy parking. Set in open space. Refreshments available.

Address: Richmond Road, Twickenham. Telephone (01) 892 5115.

The history of guns

Guns large and small, deadly and even beautiful, from medieval times to the rocket age

A unique tent-shaped building, designed by John Nash in 1820 and called the Rotunda, houses this impressive collection of artillery. It was begun by Captain (later Lieutenant-General Sir William) Congreve in 1778.

The museum forecourt bristles with many guns of different types and nationalities. Inside the Rotunda the exhibits are arranged in chronological sections. The earliest gun, called a 'bombard', dates from around 1320, is 15 inches in diameter and made of wrought iron. You can also see a breech-loading wrought-iron gun raised in 1836 from the fifteenth-century ship *Mary Rose*, which sank off Spithead.

The many specimens range through the development of artillery from wrought iron to cast iron, through muzzle-loading and breech-loading, spherical cannon-balls to cylindrical fused shells, through smooth bores to rifled bores (spiral grooving). Early sidearms lead on to sophisticated machine-guns.

One of the most impressive shells on show is a huge specimen three feet in diameter, which was fired from Mallet's mortar, weighing 42 tons. Its maximum range was more than one and a half miles.

There are also some highly decorative guns captured in India, but the most exotic-looking is a Burmese bronze gun cast in the form of a dragon.

There are many guns dating from both World Wars; one of them, a 25-pounder field gun made in 1943, was 'retired' from service with the Royal Artillery in 1967.

In the Exhibition Room there is a variety of armour, crossbows, models of battles and relics, and an exhibit showing how the Thunderbird ground-to-air guided missile was deployed and launched.

Here too are Congreve's original rocket cases and launcher of 1808.

The Royal Artillery Regimental Museum is concerned with the Regiment itself, its personnel, uniforms, medals, battle honours and its roles in peace and war, and is in the Old Royal Military Academy, Woolwich Common.

Practical details: The Museum of Artillery is open from April to October; Monday to Friday, 10 am to 12.45 pm and 2 to 5 pm; Saturday 10 am to 12 noon and 2 to 5 pm; and Sunday 2 to 5 pm. The hours are the same for the winter months, except that closing time is 4 pm.

The Royal Artillery Regimental Museum is open Monday to Friday from 10 am to 12.30 pm and 2 to 4 pm, all year round. Free admission to both. Nearest British Rail station is Woolwich Arsenal (SR). Use buses 53, 54, 75 or 122A to the Rotunda, and 122, 161 or 161A to the Royal Artillery Regimental Museum. Easy parking.
Address: The Rotunda, Repository Road, Woolwich SE18 4JJ. Telephone (01) 854 2424, extension 385.

THE MUSEUM OF LONDON

The pride and pageantry of a great city

The capital's history runs deep and wide . . . from the head of a Roman god to the Blitz and the Festival of Britain

London has always been proud of itself and its history. One of its newer sources of pride is the fine £7 million Museum of London building, which was opened by the Queen in 1976, and is one of the City's biggest attractions. In 1978 it was joint winner of the Museum of the Year award.

The museum tells the capital's long and fascinating story from prehistoric times to the present day, using the latest display and lighting techniques and offering many surprises.

The museum's London Wall site is so-called because the street follows the route of the northern part of the wall round the old Roman city of

Londinium. One surviving section, next door to the museum, can be clearly seen from a window looking down from the Roman exhibits.

Almost the first item in this chronological survey is a reconstructed cross-section of 20 feet of the ground below a nineteenth-century City cellar, showing how the archaeological deposits of 2000 years have accumulated.

London's story really began in Roman times, about AD 43, when Claudius's legions built a bridge across the Thames and settlements grew up at either end of it. Among the Roman finds on show are many ordinary domestic articles, but also perfectly preserved sculptures from the Temple of Mithras, uncovered in the City in 1954. There are also spearheads, legionaries' tombstones and part of a Roman ship found at Blackfriars.

How the Romans lived can be seen from life-size reconstructions of two dining-rooms and a kitchen. The wall paintings and furniture are modern copies, but the pottery, glass, tableware and cutlery are all authentic; the beautiful mosaic floor is real too, having been excavated in 1869 near Mansion House.

Look out among the Roman exhibits for a tile inscribed (in Latin, of course) by a brickmaker during manufacture: *For the past fortnight Austalis has been wandering off on his own every day* — an intriguing message.

The period from William the Conqueror onwards has afforded excellent scope for the professional model-makers, notably the White Tower of the Tower of London, and

Opposite: The ornate Lord Mayor's coach at the Museum of London.

Top: The White Tower, one of many skilful period reconstructions on display.

Above: Original shopfronts re-created at the Museum of London, joint winner of the 1978 Museum of the Year Award.

old St Paul's, the Gothic cathedral which preceded Wren's great building and was burned down in 1666.

The Great Fire of London is the subject of the museum's son-et-lumière feature — this goes through its impressive cycle every 10 minutes. A 12-foot-square model of the City and its timbered houses begins to glow in one corner, and this slowly spreads until the whole city is engulfed in flames . . . the wind whips clouds across the night sky . . . smoke from the blaze spirals skywards . . . All this against the background of diarist Samuel Pepys's eye-witness account, the cries of distressed house-holders, the crash of falling buildings and the crackle of flames. Even puffs of hot air issue from vents above visitors' heads. The museum's designers have striven to give each historical period display its own individual atmosphere. The Georgian London display, for example, takes its cue from the eighteenth-century architecture of Ranelagh Pleasure Gardens — a theme which contrasts strongly with the original Newgate Prison doors on show.

Behind these doors, incidentally, are the authentic wooden walls of debtors' cells from the Wellclose Square lock-up, covered with the elegantly carved names of inmates. Sombre reminders of the rough justice of the time are the whipping post nearby and the iron corpse cage in which criminals' bodies were displayed after execution.

There are several reconstructed room interiors worth seeing, including a panelled room with four-poster bed, chairs, chest and rocking-horse.

One of the most spectacular of the treasures in the Tudor section is the Cheapside Hoard — a collection of late sixteenth-century jewellery including necklaces, ear-rings, brooches and hair ornaments excavated in the City. They are thought to have been the stock-in-trade of a Jacobean jeweller, who buried them under the floor of his shop during an outbreak of the Plague in 1603.

You can see several Victorian shops — a tailor's, pharmacy, tobacconist's, draper's — which have all been reconstructed. There is a small public-house bar, correct in detail, and a late nineteenth-century Board School classroom, complete with desks, cane, blackboard and slates. This illustrates the first real attempt to provide education for all in an era unhappily characterised by squalor and ignorance.

Yet the grimness of those times was lightened by much jollity in the living theatre. Tribute is paid to the music hall and serious theatre with life-size figures of the clown Joseph Grimaldi, actors Edmund Kean and Henry Irving, and, from the music hall, Kitty Lord and George Robey. All the figures are dressed in the artistes' real-life costumes.

London's expansion as a commercial and business centre is acknowledged by such exhibits as ship models, posters and photographs of the coming suburbia, the Underground and the railways.

Then into the twentieth century, with a host of many oddly, even outrageously designed items, including 'art deco' clocks and toilet utensils. Also — one of the museum's many surprises — the famous ornate bronzed lift gates and panels which were once a feature of Selfridge's (from 1928). You can see the medals that were awarded to campaigners by the votes-for-women movement, together with posters, banners and an iron chain which they used to secure themselves to railings of the House of Commons as a gesture of protest.

Many memories will be stirred at the sight of 1920s and 1930s ephemera, such as theatre programmes, a cut-away model of an air-liner, old gramophone, candlestick telephone, model tram, and even a Ford car — a real one. Here and there can be seen other once-familiar street sights: a coster's barrow, knife-grinder's cart, bread cart, barrel organ and a hansom cab.

More sombre is the collection centred on the London Blitz early in World War II — the Anderson air-raid shelter, the nightly resort of many hundreds of thousands of Londoners, a host of photographs of damaged buildings — and even a pile of debris.

After the war, in 1951, came the Festival of Britain, with its explosion of colour, pageantry and novel design which symbolised a collective throwing-off of wartime austerity. The Festival South Bank site and buildings can be seen in model form here.

Pageantry in one form or another is a feature of every Londoner's life, and the exhibition ends on this colourful note. For the first time, the Lord Mayor of London's magnificent red and gilt state coach has been put on public display, and it is moved out of the museum only for the Lord Mayor's Show every November.

The coach was built in 1757, and is displayed over a shallow sheet of water so that the wood will not become too dry and warp. It affords a fine close-up view, particularly of the paintings on

In this ingenious model, the glow of the Great Fire gradually spreads to envelop London.

the side panels by Cipriani.

Nearby is a room devoted to special exhibitions. A programme of lunchtime lectures is held.

Practical details: Open Tuesday to Saturday from 10 am to 6 pm, and on Sunday from 2 to 6 pm. Free admission. Disabled visitors are welcome, but they should telephone for easy access directions. Nearby Underground stations are St Paul's, Barbican, Moorgate and Mansion House. Use buses 8, 22, 25 or 501 to Newgate Street or Cheapside; 6, 9, 9A, 11, 15, 502 or 513 to St Paul's; 4, 191 or 279A to Barbican. Refreshments available.

Address: London Wall EC2Y 5HN. Telephone (01) 600 3699.

MUSEUM OF MANKIND

The life and culture of different peoples

Societies on a small scale, depicted through exhibitions drawn from 800,000 items

The Museum of Mankind is the British Museum's Department of Ethnography. With a few notable exceptions, there are no permanent displays but a series of long-running, temporary exhibitions, all of which show aspects of the life and culture of small-scale societies throughout the world.

Exhibitions are mounted which show some of the most famous or important pieces from the museum's 800,000 items. Among them can be seen items from the collection of Sir Hans Sloane, an eighteenth-century President of the Royal Society, whose bequest formed the basis of the British Museum's collections. Also on display is the famous early sixteenth-century casting of the head of the Queen Mother from the Nigerian kingdom of Benin, two ivory leopards from Benin, an Aztec double-headed snake overlaid with turquoise and shell mosaic from Mexico, and a gold badge worn by royal attendants in Ashanti. Ethnographic films are shown on most days. Researchers may consult the department's library and the reserve collections.

Practical details: Open Monday to Saturday from 10 am to 5 pm, and on Sunday from 2.30 to 6 pm. Free admission. Nearby Underground stations are Piccadilly Circus and Green Park. Use buses 3, 6, 12, 14, 15, 19, 22, 25 or 38.

Address: 6 Burlington Gardens W1X 2EX. Telephone (01) 437 2224/8.

Recent exhibitions have included African Textiles, Hawaii, Ashanti Goldweights, and Captain Cook in the South Seas.

NAAFI HISTORICAL COLLECTION

Serving those who served in the war

For the fighting forces of the past, memories of the days of 'a tea and a wad'

For servicemen, past and present, the name of NAAFI — short for Navy, Army and Air Force Institutes — stirs up many memories. NAAFI operates canteens and bars and acts as 'general store' in Service camps, and some of these memories will be recaptured in this small but rapidly growing collection of relics from the past.

The original World War II crockery, bearing the NAAFI crest, is there, though the museum had quite a struggle to find any in existence. Cutlery (with holes in the handles for identification) and plastic tokens used by troops in France, Egypt, Cyprus and Berlin can be seen, together with price lists, recipe books, vases and teapots.

One ingenious early utensil, used in the '30s, was the Codd bottle — named after its inventor. It contained a glass marble in the top, thus acting as a valve to keep the 'fizz' of aerated drinks in. The one displayed was found by a skin diver in Portland Harbour.

One case shows all the medals which could have been — and often were — won by wartime NAAFI personnel, and the Institute's own Gallantry Award,

which was often won by NAAFI girls for bravery in air raids. One RASC/EFI officer, Capt Thomas Shannon, won the Military Cross (he already held the Military Medal) in Crete in World War II. The EFI, or Expeditionary Forces Institute, is NAAFI's uniformed branch in time of emergency.

The 'world's only floating brewery', RN Amenity Ship *Menestheus* (11,000 tons), which used to serve the Navy with beer and entertainment in the Far East around the end of the war, is recalled with photographs and documents. Also on show is a cheque for £10 million — the final repayment of a loan from the Treasury for the Institute's expansion in World War II. One wartime plaque thanks NAAFI for its gift in 1941 of a Spitfire called, appropriately enough, *Counter Attack*.

There are many photographs of the activities of the Institute's immediate predecessor, the Navy and Army Canteen Board, in World War I. Also of its own work in World War II, with a range of badges, plaques and signs from canteens in many parts of the world, where NAAFI lived up to its motto, *Servitor Servientium* — 'We serve those who serve'.

Practical details: Imperial Court is expected to be closed throughout 1979 for renovations and should re-open early in 1980. The museum will be open to visitors by appointment. Enquiries may be made by telephone. Nearby Underground stations are Kennington and Vauxhall. Use buses 95, 133 or 159 to Kennington Park, or 3, 109, 155, 159 or 172 to Kennington Cross.

Address: Imperial Court, Kennington Lane SE11 5QX. Telephone (01) 735 1200 extension 626.

The British Army at war

The story of hand-held weapons and the Army's role, with relics from famous battlefields

Almost the first exhibit encountered at the National Army Museum, is also one of the oddest: the skeleton of Napoleon's favourite charger, Marengo. The horse was called after the battle of that name and is thought to have been ridden by Napoleon at Waterloo.

This museum, situated appropriately near to the Royal Hospital, Chelsea (see page 126), home of the famous Pensioners, was opened by the Queen in 1971.

The new Weapon Gallery, opened in 1978, is on the ground floor, and represents the first serious attempt by any museum to trace the development of hand-held weapons used by the British soldier from the Middle Ages to the present.

The earliest weapon on show is a longbow from the wreck of Henry VIII's ship *Mary Rose*, sunk in 1525. A sword, broken down to its main components, shows how each part developed until in 1908 the ideal sword was achieved, though it was of course too late to be of use in modern actions.

The development of gunlocks is explained through 'exploded' line drawings and models. Comparisons of the accuracy and range of half-a-dozen weapons are made — from the smooth-bore musket of 1580 to the 1903 Short Magazine Lee Enfield. In addition to personal weapons there are displays featuring machine-guns, grenades, mortars and light anti-tank weapons.

A street scene tableau shows models carrying a range of weapons currently in use against urban terrorists. There are films and slides showing how weapons were carried and used. Many weapons are shown in circular and semi-circular cases so that they can be studied from all angles. There is an electronic shooting gallery for visitors to test their marksmanship.

On the first floor, nearly a hundred cases of armour, uniforms, weapons, battle plans and the personal belongings of famous military leaders tell the story of the army from its earliest days, when the first organized formation, the Yeoman of the Guard, was founded by Henry VII in 1485, up

A multitude of fighting weapons, of every kind.

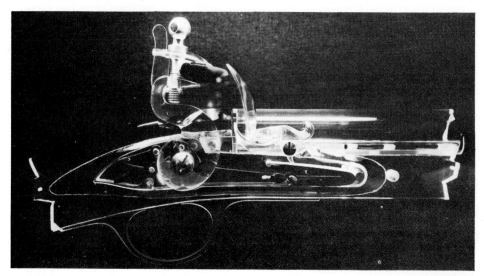

A perspex model reveals the internal mechanisms of the flintlock.

to 1914.

An exhibit not to be missed near the start of the chronological tour is the crimson horse housing, richly embroidered in gold and silver, which was used by the first Duke of Marlborough, victor of Blenheim. A battle plan of Blenheim is also on show.

From other battlefields have come General Wolfe's crimson sash and the faded cloak he was wrapped in at his death, and the waist sash worn by Sir John Moore when mortally wounded at Corunna in 1809.

The Duke of Wellington, hero of Waterloo, is remembered by his field-marshal's uniform, including cocked hat, and such personal items as his shaving mirror and the barometer he carried on campaigns in Spain and Portugal. There are also a ticket and programme for his huge funeral in 1852 (see St Paul's Cathedral Crypt, page 155). Among the sombre reminders of Waterloo are the surgeon's saw which was used to amputate the leg of the Earl of Uxbridge, and the bloodstained glove and handkerchief. A shako (head-dress) on display contains a musket-ball hole made during the fighting.

Among the relics of the Crimean War is a buckskin pouch used by Field-Marshal Lord Raglan for his despatches to the War Office, and his telescope; also the cloak worn by Captain Nolan in the Charge of the Light Brigade. It was Nolan who conveyed the fatal order to charge to Lord Lucan, and he himself was killed. The charge, immortalized by Tennyson in his famous poem, was a military blunder because it was made in the wrong direction — the result of a misunderstood order from Lord Cardigan. Also on show are a bugle, helmets and equipment captured from the Russians, and a signpost from the Crimea saying 'Balaklava'.

Florence Nightingale, 'the lady with the lamp' who tended the wounded from the Crimea, is represented by her decorations, medals and jewellery, among which is a brooch from Queen Victoria inscribed: 'To Miss Florence Nightingale as a mark of esteem and gratitude for her devotion towards the Queen's brave soldiers. From Victoria R., 1855.'

Of the many causes of war, surely one of the most unusual was the reason for the Indian Mutiny of 1857, illustrated here with rifles and cartridges. In those days the end of a cartridge for the Enfield rifle had to be bitten off before loading. It was lubricated with animal fat. Pig fat would have been offensive to the Muslim and cow fat repugnant to the Hindu. The unconfirmed rumour that the grease of one of these animals was used, was the last in a chain of events which led to a rebellion against the British.

One of the bravest actions in the nineteenth century was in the Zulu Wars. In 1879, for twelve hours, 140 men of the 24th Regiment defended their small post against 4,000 Zulus at Rorke's Drift. One of several Victoria Crosses awarded for this is on show, together with the Zulu chief's head-dress, weapons and shield. A model illustrates the battle.

Also worth seeing is the imposing table centrepiece, in solid silver, consisting of trees and animals, which was presented to the 65th Regiment to commemorate 20 years' service in New Zealand from 1845 to 1865. From the Boer War come many souvenirs issued at the time to mark the relief of Mafeking and its hero, Robert Baden-Powell (see Baden-Powell House, page 9).

The Story of the Army exhibition concludes with World War I items, including a uniform of the period and the warning order from the Prime Minister, Mr Asquith, for the 'precautionary stage' to be adopted by the forces a week before war was declared in 1914.

On the top floor are the uniform and art galleries. The former describes, with colourful displays of uniforms, head-dress and decorations, how army clothing has progressed from the civilian dress of the fifteenth century, through the elaborately colourful in the eighteenth century, to the more practical, if more sober-looking, khaki battledress of the twentieth. There is an interesting display in one case, which shows an officer's bed (capable of being converted into a chair in daytime), his box of silver toilet items, utensils and travelling canteen. Even in battle, there was a place for comfortable living. Two other memorable features are the batons, insignia and decorations of five field-marshals, including Lords Roberts and Kitchener.

In the art gallery are portraits of some of the great military leaders, including works by Gainsborough and Reynolds. There is a small picture by Edward Penny of the Marquis of Granby speaking to a sick soldier and his family after battle. The Marquis was known as a particularly kindly commander in the eighteenth century, and grateful soldiers who served under him named public houses after him. Many still bear his name.

Practical details: Open Monday to Saturday from 10 am to 5.30 pm, and on Sunday from 2 to 5.30 pm. Free admission. Nearest Underground station is Sloane Square. Use buses 11, 19, 22, 39 or 137.

Address: Royal Hospital Road, Chelsea SW3 4HT. Telephone (01) 730 0717.

THE NATIONAL GALLERY

The art treasures of the Nation

From 2,000 pictures, a selection of those that should not be missed

The National Gallery, built to the design of William Wilkins, was opened to the public in 1838. Only the classical facade remains unchanged. In its eternal struggle for more accommodation, there has been continual growth.

Today the National Gallery's entire collection numbers well over 2,000 pictures. From its own nominations of pictures to see, the author has made a personal choice of 17. These are as follows:

Botticelli (*c* 1450-1510), *Mars and Venus*. A masterpiece on the symbolic theme of 'love conquers war'. Mars lies back exhausted while Venus looks on complacently and satyrs steal away with Mars's helmet and lance.

Constable (1776-1837), *The Hay Wain*. The evocative painting, set in Suffolk, that brought fame to England's greatest landscape painter in 1824, when it was exhibited at the Paris Salon. The scene, on the River Stour, is still recognizable.

Correggio (1494-1534), *Mercury instructing Cupid*. What was then the new medium of oil paint is exercised to brilliant effect in this picture of three nude figures.

Jan Van Eyck (*c* 1385-1441), *Jan*

Belshazzar's Feast, by Rembrandt.

Arnolfini and his Wife. A famous double portrait, notable not only for its excellent technique, but for the remarkable precision and abundance of detail. Painted in Bruges in 1434.

Gainsborough (1727-88), *The Morning Walk*. Another double portrait. A romantic picture by the famous court and landscape painter of a newly married, fashionably dressed couple. Interesting for its ingenious effects of light and shade. Purchased from Lord Rothschild in 1954.

Hogarth (1697-1764), *Marriage à la Mode*. Hogarth's energies as a painter and engraver were largely directed to social satire. This series of six paintings tells the unhappy story of a marriage between a wealthy merchant's daughter and a young viscount.

Holbein (the Younger) (1497/8-1543), *The Duchess of Milan*. Holbein was court painter to Henry VIII, for whom he made this picture. The duchess, the widowed Christina of Denmark, was supposed to marry Henry, but the match did not materialize. Here she wears mourning.

Leonardo da Vinci (1452-1519), *The*

Virgin and Child with St Anne and St John the Baptist. The famous cartoon was presented to the gallery in 1962 by the National Art-Collections Fund, who had purchased it from the Royal Academy for £800,000 after organizing a successful public appeal. It is an intensely moving drawing in black chalk heightened with white. *The Virgin of the Rocks:* another beautiful work by Leonardo, depicting the Holy Family in a strange grotto-like setting. The effect is almost dream-like.

Rembrandt (1606-1669), *Belshazzar's Feast.* Signed 'Rembrand./f 163(?)'. The last digit of the date is lost, but the picture was probably painted soon after 1635. Its subject is from Daniel, Chapter V, 1-4. The painting came to the National Gallery in 1964.

Renoir (1841-1919), *Les Parapluies.* No wet day could be more captivating than in Renoir's picture. Changes in technique and in the styles of clothing worn by the umbrella-clutching group suggest the painting was completed over several years.

Rubens (1577-1640), *Le Chapeau de paille.* A pleasingly colourful portrait of Rubens' sister-in-law, Susanne Fourmet, who stares calmly out with wide dark eyes from under a black Spanish beaver hat.

Titian (1489-1576), *Bacchus and Ariadne.* Bacchus, with nymphs, fauns and satyrs, takes Ariadne by surprise. One of the gallery's gems, richly complex and full of movement, it has been described as 'one of the most amazing pictorial compositions in existence'.

Turner (1775-1851), *Fighting Téméraire.* A veteran of Trafalgar, the *Téméraire* was in 1838 towed from Sheerness to London for breaking up.

Turner captured the scene in this symphony of colour, now his most famous picture, which was exhibited the following year at the Royal Academy.

Velazquez (1599-1660), *The Toilet of Venus* (The Rokeby Venus). The female nude hardly appears in seventeenth-century Spanish art, except in Velazquez's work. His Venus steps out of myth into reality, with human-like flesh tints that give this picture an admirable warmth. Called the 'Rokeby' Venus because it was once kept at Rokeby in Yorkshire.

Veronese (*c* 1528-88), *Family of Darius before Alexander.* An elaborate and detailed picture portraying the appearance before a victorious but gracious Alexander the Great of the defeated Persian emperor, Darius. Deservedly one of Veronese's most famous works.

Finally, a mystery picture, the *Wilton Diptych,* a beautiful work by an unknown fourteenth-century artist of the early English or French school. In the left-hand panel, against a richly gilded background, Richard II (for whom it was painted) kneels in the standing company of St Edmund, St Edward the Confessor and St John the Baptist. In the right, the Virgin, attended by angels, presents the Holy Child.

Practical details: Open Monday to Saturday from 10 am to 6 pm, and on Sunday from 2 to 6 pm. Free admission. Nearest British Rail station is Charing Cross (SR). Nearby Underground stations are Embankment and Trafalgar Square. Use buses 3, 6, 11, 12, 15, 24, 29, 53, 77 or 88. Refreshments available. **Address:** Trafalgar Square WC2N 5DN. Telephone (01) 839 3321.

**NATIONAL
MARITIME
MUSEUM
AND OLD
ROYAL
OBSERVATORY**

Hearts of Oak

**Where Britain's seafaring history is
enshrined . . . with relics of Nelson
and Cook, a host of navigational
instruments, ship models galore —
and even a real paddle-tug**

No museum in London has a nobler
setting than the National Maritime
Museum. To stand and gaze down
upon it and across the Thames
beyond, from the old Royal
Observatory which breaks the skyline
half a mile away across Greenwich
Park, is to enjoy a rare sight indeed.
It is fitting that this museum of the sea
should itself be rich in historical
associations. Kings and queens lived
in its precincts, Sir Francis Drake was
knighted nearby, and so was Sir
Francis Chichester; the old *Great
Eastern* steamship was built opposite,
at Millwall, and the *Mayflower,* in
which the Pilgrim Fathers sailed to
America, at Rotherhithe.

The first building to visit is the East
Wing, which covers Merchant Navy
history up to 1945, and Royal Navy
history to World War II. Photographs
and engravings illustrate what life was
like in emigrant ships (often cramped
and squalid). A relief chart of the
North Atlantic, marked with timber
ship routes, shows the 'hilly' nature of
the Atlantic's ocean floor. An
exhibition, 'Fifty years of the small

British merchant sailing-ship',
contains diagrams, pictures and
contemporary photographs.

There is a reconstruction of the
foredeck of a small (fictitious) ketch,
Annie May, with genuine anchor,
windlass, pumphandle, jib sheet and
bell, which came from ketches of
similar design.

Among the many models is one of the
last square-rigged merchant ship, the
Waterwitch (1871); she made her last
voyage in 1936. There are several very
large models, including *City of
Benares* (1936), and the 810-ton steam
trawler *Princess Elizabeth,* launched
in the 1950s.

Various kinds of deep-sea fishing are
demonstrated with models, and there
is a prize-winning exhibit of a
quadruple-expansion steam-engine.
Downstairs, in the Arctic Gallery, is
original material, including sledges,
clothing, equipment, utensils,
chronometers — and Bibles —
discovered after Sir John Franklin's

tateful Arctic expedition of 1845, when attempts to find human survivors failed.

Through the colonnade will be found the Queen's House, described as the most beautiful house in the country. It was designed for Anne of Denmark, wife of James I, and completed for Charles I's queen, Henrietta-Maria. The Great Hall, a 40-foot cube, was the work of Inigo Jones. His 'tulip' staircase is notable for being the first open-well staircase in the country: it spirals round space instead of a central support. The large ceiling painting is the work of Sir James Thornhill's pupils.

Museum exhibits in the Queen's House cover the Tudor and Stuart periods. There is an impressive collection of scale models of seventeenth-century warships, and of portraits of Queen Elizabeth and luminaries such as Drake and Essex, Samuel Pepys, James I, and Inigo Jones himself. There are also many paintings of naval battles.

A wall display features the seventeenth- century Swedish ship *Wasa,* which sank on her maiden voyage in 1628, and was raised from the bottom of the sea in Stockholm in 1961.

Along the second colonnade and into the West Wing. Here the Caird galleries tell the story of maritime history from 1688 to 1815. The biggest feature, and the most astonishing, is in the New Neptune Hall: a full-sized paddle-tug, *Reliant,* which is in working order and complete with turning engine and creaking paddlewheel. Dated 1907, the tug is 90 feet long and 20 feet wide, and forms the centrepiece of a display on the development of the steamship.

Visitors are at liberty to walk the decks, peer through glass panels in the sides to inspect the crew's quarters, and stand in the engine room.

Several other vessels are on show: *Donola,* of 1893, a private motor yacht built for Mr Alfred Palmer of Huntley & Palmer; *Miss Britain III,* which in 1933 became the first boat ever to touch 100 mph, and was for some years the fastest single-engined boat in the world.

In the neighbouring Barge House, newly restored and refurbished, are several ceremonial barges. The most impressive is the State Barge designed by William Kent for Frederick, Prince of Wales, father of George III, in 1732. It has recently been beautifully regilded and restored. The museum's oldest barge (dating from 1689) is on show. It belonged to Queen Mary II, and was used by King George V as recently as 1919 for a Peace Procession on the Thames.

Two other barges on show were used by Commissioners of the Navy in the eighteenth century — the heyday also of Thames watermen, who with their craft and uniforms are also acknowledged here.

Themes of various exhibitions in the New Neptune Hall include the development of the boat, the evolution from sail to steam, services to shipping, and boat-building.

The Cook Gallery pays informative tribute to Captain James Cook, the greatest navigator in history, and his three historic voyages. There are displays of his observation instruments, a finely-made model of his ship *Endeavour,* a cannon which had been thrown overboard to lighten the ship in 1770, and part of her sternpost. Cook's tragic murder by

natives in Hawaii is remembered in two paintings by Bryne and Zoffany. Near the entrance to the Nelson Gallery is an actual-size replica of a standard 32-pounder muzzle-loading cannon — a weapon typical of those used by the Navy in the Napoleonic Wars. Inside you can see Nelson's Bible, which he took to sea in his youth, a tableau of relics loaned by relatives of Nelson, some cabin furniture from his ship, the *Victory*, including his wash-stand and writing desk. There is a display of Nelson's uniforms, including a bloodstained waistcoat and the undress coat which he was wearing at the time of his death. The bullet-hole through the left shoulder, made by a musket shot from a French ship, is clearly visible. In the Navigation Room are maps and charts from the fifteenth and sixteenth centuries, timekeepers, telescopes, compasses, and speed and depth-measuring devices. Individual exhibits include John Harrison's

In the new Barge House at the National Maritime Museum.

marine timekeepers made between 1729 and 1735. Harrison's No 4 chronometer proved accurate enough for longitude to be calculated on the basis of time at sea, and it won him a prize of £20,000 from the Government. The *Bounty* watch was issued in 1787 to Captain Bligh for the voyage of the ship to the West Indies, to plant breadfruit. The expedition is described, and among the relics are the master's telescope, a pigtail of the last surviving mutineer, John Adams, Captain Bligh's sword, pipe and reading glass.

In 1647, the coasts of Australia, Tasmania and New Zealand appeared on a map for the first time. The large Dutch terrestrial globe shows these with the unexplored east coasts left blank.

The East Wing of the museum contains a centre for creative activities

Left: Mermaid decoration for King Frederick's Barge, 1731, now carefully restored.
Bottom: An imaginative sea creature on the Barge.

for children called 'The Half Deck'. It is fitted out like a passenger liner and contains a studio for modelling, photography, painting and drawing, based on ideas stimulated by touring the museum galleries.

Practical details: The museum is open from Easter to November, Monday to Saturday from 10 am to 6 pm and on Sunday from 2.30 to 6 pm. The hours are the same for the rest of the year except that it closes at 5 pm from Monday to Friday. The studio is available to organised school groups (who must book in advance) from Tuesday to Friday in term time, and for club members from Tuesday to Thursday in the holidays. Free admission. Nearest British Rail station is Maze Hill (SR). Use buses 108 or 177. Open spaces nearby. Refreshments available.

Address: Romney Road, Greenwich SE10 9NF. Telephone (01) 858 4422.

OLD ROYAL OBSERVATORY

Sir Christopher Wren built the old Royal Observatory for Charles II for the purpose of solving the problem of longitude for seamen, whose perennial difficulty was in pinpointing their position at sea once out of sight of land.

The first Astronomer-Royal, John Flamsteed, lived in what is now Flamsteed House — 'built for the Observator's habitation and a little for Pompe', wrote Wren — and visitors can tour the living quarters, which are still furnished. Upstairs in the

Octagon Room and adjoining galleries are large displays of early astronomical and navigational instruments, sundials and clocks. The red time ball above a turret on the roof of the house drops down its mast every day at 1 pm precisely, as a time signal for ships on the Thames — a custom that has continued since 1833. Behind the house is the Meridian Building, which contains the original and replica transit telescopes. These fixed a line in the heavens against which movement of sun and stars could be measured, and many of the instruments used by successive Astronomers-Royal are in their original settings. One of these is Airy's Transit Instrument, which was used to define the Prime Meridian, Longitude 0°, recognized by international agreement in 1884 and throughout the world ever since. The last regular observation with the transit telescope was made in 1954, and it remains in working order. The Meridian is marked on the ground in the courtyard, where it is possible to bestride the line and thus stand in both Eastern and Western hemispheres at once.

Several interesting telescopes can be seen in the Dyson Gallery, including Herschel's 10-foot reflector (1805) and his 20-foot version of 1820. Sir William Herschel was George III's astronomer, and in 1781 he discovered the planet Uranus.

Practical details: Open Easter to November, Monday to Saturday from 10 am to 6 pm, and on Sunday from 2.30 to 6 pm. The rest of the year it opens at 10 am daily and closes half-an-hour before the park, perhaps as early as 4.30 pm. Free admission. Nearest British Rail station is Maze Hill (SR). Use buses 53, 54, or 75. Open spaces nearby.
Address: Romney Road, Greenwich SE10 9NF. Telephone (01) 858 1167.

THE ROYAL NAVAL COLLEGE

This is separate from the National Maritime Museum, but is convenient enough for visits to include both in one trip. The college was designed by Sir Christopher Wren as a Royal Hospital for Seamen alongside the existing King's House, and it became a college for naval officers in 1873. Nelson's body lay in state in the Painted Hall over Christmas 1805, before being carried by state barge to St Paul's Cathedral. The hall is magnificently decorated, with lavish ceiling and wall paintings by Sir James Thornhill. These feature William and Mary in symbolic scenes, which also include such famous contributors to scientific knowledge as Newton, Tycho Brahe, Archimedes and Copernicus.

Thornhill himself appears in the painting on the stairs. He is supposedly acknowledging the Royal Family with his right hand, while the other is open for more money. He thought himself very badly paid for his work, which took him 19 years to complete.

The Hall, chapel and undercroft are open to the public, but there is no access to the rest of the college.

Practical details: Open daily (not Thursday) from 2.30 to 5.30 pm. Free admission. Nearest British Rail station is Maze Hill (SR). Use buses 108 or 177. Open spaces nearby. Refreshments available.
Address: King William Walk SE10 9NN. Telephone (01) 858 2154.

NATIONAL MUSEUM
OF LABOUR HISTORY

Labour's past

Trade union banners, relics of historic strikes and the Peterloo Massacre — and even Sir Harold Wilson's pipe

When the Prime Minister of the day, Harold Wilson, opened this museum in 1975, he himself contributed an exhibit to it — one of his famous pipes. It joined that of the first Labour Premier of the postwar era, Mr (later Earl) Attlee.

Whatever one's politics, the rise of the Labour and trade union movements over the past 150 years is an important part of history. In this museum, with trade union banners colourfully decking the walls, one can read newspaper accounts of events like the Peterloo Massacre in 1819, and demonstrations for the release of the Tolpuddle martyrs. These were six agricultural labourers who, in 1834, had been sentenced to transportation for forming a 'combination' to resist wage cuts. Public pressure led to their release.

Tribute is paid to some early radicals, such as Tom Paine, the eighteenth-century revolutionary. A first edition copy of his *Rights of Man* is there, along with Paine's death mask, a lock of his hair and the table on which he wrote the famous book. One of the prime movers in the Repeal of the Corn Laws (tariffs which bore heavily on the poor) was Richard Cobden, and his table and chair, which once belonged to the anarchist Prince Peter Kropotkin, are on show.

The foundation of the Trades Union Congress (which, with Tower Hamlets Council, has played a leading role in sponsoring the museum) is described, and a copy of the original notice of the first meeting organised in 1868 can be seen; also relics of the Paris Commune in 1871, including a bullet, gun cotton, oats and a biscuit.

Other exhibits recall three famous strikes of the late nineteenth century: the match girls, the London dockers (over the dockers 'tanner'), and the gas workers.

There are many interesting mementoes of Labour luminaries: a John Bright tile, a Cobden figure, jugs marking the First Reform Act of 1832 and Keir Hardie's earthenware miner's lamp, which he used when he worked opening doors for pit ponies. Material connected with the Cooperative Movement, Socialist Sunday Schools, Labour Governments, the Spanish Civil War and Women's Emancipation can also be seen.

Practical details: Open Tuesday to Friday from 11 am to 4.30 pm. Free admission, though contributions are welcome. Nearest Underground station is Mile End. Use buses 5, 15, 23 or 40.

Address: Limehouse Town Hall, Commercial Road, London E14. NOTE: In late 1979 or early 1980 the museum is due to move to larger premises at Mile End Baths, Mile End Road, London E1.

NATIONAL MUSICAL MUSEUM

Exotic instruments

See self-playing violins and a small automatic orchestra among this fascinating collection of mechanical instruments

In the improbable setting of a disused church near the gasholder on the north side of Kew Bridge is the National Musical Museum — an archaic collection of 200 musical instruments, a large number of which are automatic. The curator, Mr Frank Holland, calls it his 'zoo full of rare and exotic animals, all with their different colours and cries'.

More keeper than curator, he lovingly demonstrates his charges to visitors every summer Saturday and Sunday afternoon. He is also in the forefront of a battle to move his museum — too cold in winter — to a 'Science Theatre' behind the mansion of the late Sir David Salomons at Tunbridge Wells, which houses the costliest automatic philharmonic reproducing pipe organ and orchestrion ever installed in Britain.

Many of the instruments at Brentford have come from palaces, public houses or amusement arcades (some complete with coin-in-the-slot attachments) or from private individuals. Player pianos, which produce music by means of air drawn in through perforations in rolls of paper, self-playing violins, orchestrions (mechanical organs), disc

A self-playing violin, invented early this century.

musical boxes — at least a dozen will be played and described in detail during a two hours' visit.

There are an Edison phonograph, to which visitors can listen through rubber ear-tubes, a Regina disc musical box, and a variety of automatic pianos which reproduce music in the manner of the virtuoso who may have recorded it on the rolls (the museum has over 20,000 rolls for various instruments).

Mr Holland's collection is the result of the Victorians' and Edwardians' passion and genius for mechanization — coupled, of course, with his own zeal for conservation. Almost the only manual instruments are a few pianos, a busker's street barrel organ and a mighty WurliTzer.

Not content with one individual sound, the Victorians endowed some instruments with many. For example, the grandiosely named Hupfeld Animatic-Clavitist Sinfonie-Jazz Piano Model No 9, made c 1926 and rescued from an amusement arcade in Devon, yields up sounds not only of a piano but also cymbals, triangle, drums, Chinese block and saxophone. The museum has three Imhof and Mukle orchestrions. The biggest exhibit of all is the mighty WurliTzer which originally graced the Regal Cinema, Kingston-upon-Thames. The introductory recital, in February 1932, was played by Reginald Foort, who used it for BBC radio broadcasts for several years.

Today, when resident organist Joseph Seal is not performing on it, the instrument gives its own recitals, thanks to a device called the WurliTzer Automatic Reproducing Roll Player, the only one ever installed in Europe. This is used in conjunction with a Steinway grand piano which plays when the stops on the organ are opened. It is now proclaimed by many experts to be the finest-toned installation in Europe. Every imaginable instrument can be called upon, plus special effects such as klaxon horn, steamboat whistle, horses' hooves, fire-gong, surf breaking on the shore, bird whistle and door bell. Not forgetting the changing coloured lights in the glass panels — an essential feature of the old cinema organ.

In the first decade or so of this century, attempts were made for automatic instruments to emulate the playing of the violin. One model that can be heard to perfection here is the electrically-driven Violano-Virtuoso, made by the Mills Novelty Company of Chicago. It incorporates a real violin, installed horizontally, and gives out a remarkably mellow tone. This, too, is played with a player piano. Plastic wheels perform the bowing, and the stopping is done by automatic 'fingers' which flip up under the strings.

The other self-playing violin consists of three violins standing vertically in a triangle, with one string on each projecting beyond the other three, being played by a rotating circular horsehair bow.

Practical details: Visits are in the form of a talk and demonstration which begins at 2 pm on Saturday and Sunday from April to October. There is an admission charge. Nearby British Rail stations are Brentford Central (SR) and Kew Bridge (SR). Use buses 65, 116, 237, 267, E1 or E2.

Address: 368 High Street, Brentford, Middlesex TW8 0BD. Telephone (01) 560 8108.

People in paint

Eight hundred portraits of kings and queens, statesmen and those who achieved distinction in the arts and sciences

In this gallery, history springs from the pages of the text book and puts on an expressive face. It was founded in 1856 and now contains more than 5,000 likenesses of prominent people in Britain's past and present — paintings, drawings, sculpture, silhouettes and photographs.

The pictures are so numerous that only about 800 can be shown at any one time, the rest having to remain in the reserve collection, to be consulted by the public on request (and with advance notice).

The earliest documented painting from life of an English king is the small revealing portrait of Henry VII, and there is a splendid cartoon by Holbein of Henry VII and Henry VIII, which was a working drawing used as a stencil to transfer the design on to the wall of the Privy Chamber of the old Whitehall Palace. The stencil pinpricks are still visible.

There are several pictures of Elizabeth I herself, one of the most impressive showing her standing on a map of England.

The famous portrait of William Shakespeare, once owned by the Duke of Chandos, is among the first pictures to be seen. It is thought to have been painted from life, though the artist is unknown. There are several pictures of Charles I in the gallery, and of

Queen Elizabeth I, one of 800 portraits at the National Portrait Gallery.

Oliver Cromwell, who demanded of the painter, Sir Peter Lely, a picture showing 'pimples, warts & everything as you see me; otherwise I never will pay a farthing for it'.

There are a number of self-portraits, too, among them Thomas Gainsborough, Sir Joshua Reynolds and William Hogarth.

We can find pictures of eighteenth-century politicians like William Pitt and Charles James Fox, the victorious Duke of Wellington, Nelson (and his beautiful mistress, Lady Hamilton).

Two galleries are occupied by a selection from Sir Godfrey Kneller's Kit-Cat Club portraits — 43 in all — of Whig politicians painted between 1697 and 1721.

One of the most imposing paintings from the nineteenth century is of the Reformed House of Commons by Hayter. It shows more than 400 Members of Parliament, and some members of the House of Lords, listening to the moving of the address to the Crown. There are also pictures of Gladstone, Disraeli, Melbourne and other political leaders.

Phillips's famous painting of Lord Byron in Greek costume hangs among 'The Romantics', while 'The Early Victorians' include the strange triple portrait of the Brontë sisters, painted with more sensitivity than technique by their brother Branwell. In the background of this picture is the outline of an erased figure, possibly the artist himself.

Among the many Victorian men of letters and science which stare down from the walls are Carlyle, Ruskin, William Morris, Charles Darwin, Faraday and Dickens. Famous examples of Victorian womanhood include Florence Nightingale. Gilbert and Sullivan, stormy creators of the Savoy operas, now hang peacefully together, and other musical luminaries like Vaughan Williams, Delius, Elgar and Sir Thomas Beecham are represented.

Prominent twentieth-century figures shown here include a cigar-smoking Winston Churchill, a pensive figure painted by Sickert in 1928; the large painting of George V and his family by Lavery; and Annigoni's controversial portrait of Elizabeth II, painted in 1970.

Practical details: Open Monday to Friday from 10 am to 5 pm, Saturday from 10 am to 6 pm and Sunday from 2 to 6 pm. Free admission. Nearby Underground stations are Trafalgar Square and Leicester Square. Use buses 3, 6, 11, 12, 14, 15, 19, 22, 24, 29, 53, 77, 88 or 176.
Address: St Martin's Place WC2H 0HE. Telephone (01) 930 1552.

NATIONAL POSTAL MUSEUM

Every British stamp ~ and many more worldwide

Unique proof Penny Blacks among 250,000 specimens . . . a mecca for all collectors

Owned by the Post Office, this museum was built up on the R M Phillips International Grand Prix stamp collection of the reign of Queen Victoria, and the stamp archives of the Post Office itself. The museum was opened by·the Queen in 1969.

The pioneer of Uniform Penny Postage, Sir Rowland Hill, is duly acknowledged in several exhibits, including the original letter, dated 1839, which outlined his scheme. This provided for letters for any address in Britain to be paid for by the sender at a low initial rate — one penny per half-

The stamps that were never issued: the Edward VIII Coronation set.

ounce — instead of double that rate when paid for by the recipient.

A large number of original designs, which were submitted in 1839 in a Treasury contest to find a form of stamp that would defy forgery, can be seen. For the design eventually adopted, the Treasury chose a portrait of Queen Victoria drawn by Henry Corbould. It was based on the portrait of the Queen which had been engraved by William Wyon on a medal struck to mark her first visit to the City of London. This, with a frame and inscription, was used on the first stamps, the 'penny blacks', issued in May 1840.

The Queen's head was chosen because everyone was familiar with her portrait, and forgery, it was thought, would be more difficult.

The original die, engraved by Charles Heath, is on show, with several subsequent ones. The museum also has a number of unique proof sheets of the Penny Black and the largest block in the world: 43 copies of the issued stamp.

The 250,000 stamps on exhibition are set out in glass frames, and cover all British stamps issued from 1840 to the present. There is a Universal Postal Union collection of all stamps issued throughout the world since 1878. The museum also houses the unique philatelic archives of Thomas De La Rue & Company, covering the stamps printed by them for Great Britain and some 150 other countries between 1855 and 1965.

Unusual items are the forgeries made and used by clerks in the Stock Exchange Post Office about 1872-75; also the essays for the Coronation issue of King Edward VIII, and for an Anglo-French joint issue in 1940. In

The only complete proof sheet of Penny Blacks, probably the most valuable philatelic item in the world.

both cases, of course, owing to the abdication and the outbreak of war respectively, neither issue of stamps actually came out.

Every year since 1950 the Philatelic Congress of Great Britain has sponsored a national junior philatelic competition in memory of Fred J Melville, a famous collector who took pains to encourage young philatelists. He died in 1940. The prizewinners' entries and those of the runners-up have been shown in the museum since 1973.

Practical details: Open Monday to Friday from 10 am to 4.30 pm. Free admission. Nearby Underground stations are St Paul's and Moorgate. Use buses 8, 22 or 25.

Address: King Edward Street EC1A 1LP. Telephone (01) 432 3851.

NATURAL HISTORY MUSEUM

Life in close~up

All creatures great and small, from whales and dinosaurs to bees and fleas — and a lingering look at Man

The first pieces of natural history encountered here stand in the forecourt of this great cathedral-like museum: a fossilised tree trunk 300 million years old, and some huge casts of footprints of a species of dinosaur called *Megalosaurus*.

An impressive new display of dinosaurs in the Central Hall is called 'Dinosaurs and their living relatives' — among them an 85-feet-long plaster cast skeleton of *Diplodocus carnegii*, and the horned *Triceratops prorsus*, with large-scale models of the animals alongside. Exhibits show how dinosaurs are related to each other and to living animals, with specimens including modern animals, dinosaur eggs, an ichthyosaur with skeletons of its young, and the fossil bird *Archaeopteryx*. There are specimens of dinosaurs (including a head of *Tyrannosaurus rex*), fossil amphibians, plesiosaurs and flying reptiles.

In the exhibition room behind the Central Hall is a real, though dead, coelacanth — a large, strange-looking fish thought until recently to have been extinct for about 70 million years. But many coelacanths have been caught around Madagascar since the first one was found in 1938.

Off the hall is the Arachnid Gallery, which describes in fascinating detail the life stories of spiders, scorpions and mites, and shows, for example, the seven stages of web-spinning and how a spider's silk is produced. The models of the creatures, like many in the museum, are several times life-size for clarity.

Also on the ground floor is a group of the largest land animals — elephant, rhinoceros and hippopotamus; but the biggest mammal that has ever lived in the world is the blue whale — a 91-feet model stands in the Whale Hall.

Near the elephants is told the interesting story of 'Piltdown Man'. This was the discovery (which turned out to be a hoax) involving the alleged remains of an ancient man found in gravel at Piltdown, Sussex.

They were claimed by the 'finder' in 1912 to be those of early man. In 1949, however, experts using scientific 'detective' methods proved that the fragments were not from ancient man at all, nor even from Piltdown, but originated a mere 500 or 600 years ago.

A new and impressive permanent exhibition hall is devoted to 'Human Biology — an exhibition of ourselves'. This uses large models, sound and visual effects (even the fairground distorting mirrors find a place here!), films, slide shows and games. With a good deal of fun, visitors can explore the structure of the human body — its functions, organs and senses — learning in the process how we grow, how actions are controlled by the brain, how objects are recognised and how muscles work.

Several exhibits describe in easily understood detail the story of

Opposite: A baby before birth, part of the new display 'Human biology — an exhibition of ourselves'.

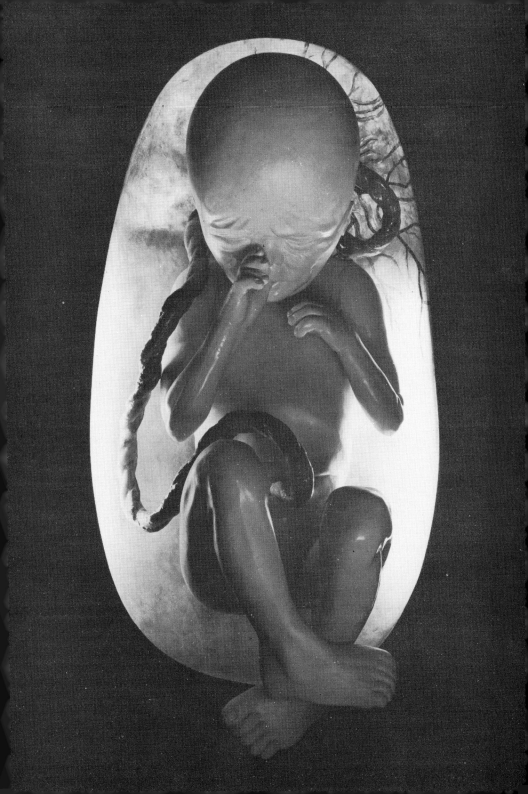

All the fascination of dinosaurs, at the Natural History Museum.

conception, pregnancy, and the way a child develops from babyhood.

Another fairly new gallery, opened in 1968, is devoted to insects. There are more insect species — about a million — than of any other kind of animal. Here you can learn how they feed, reproduce and change their shape during development.

A large recently opened exhibition, 'Introducing Ecology', is an exciting series of displays and dioramas based on a British oak woodland and a rocky seashore. It illustrates how plants, animals and other organisms react with each other and with and to their surroundings. The exhibition covers energy and the sun's role in providing it for all living things. The food chain — the eating of a plant by an animal, which is itself eaten by another animal — is demonstrated by two converted what-the-butler-saw machines.

A specially designed computer-controlled display ends the exhibition. It enables visitors to investigate a real ecological problem: how to discover the cause of severe damage to oak trees that has occurred in recent years in a particular woodland.

In the Mineral Gallery on the first floor there is a dazzling array of 7,000 rocks — precious and semi-precious stones of all kinds, including gold and platinum.

Meteorites found in hot deserts are to be seen in the adjoining Meteorite Pavilion. The largest on display weighs three-and-a-half tons, is largely iron, and was found at Cranbourne, near Melbourne, in 1854.

Near the Botany Gallery there is a huge cross-section of the Californian Big Tree, *Sequoiadendron giganteum,* which was more than 1,300 years old when cut down in 1892. Notable historical events are marked on the appropriate age rings, ranging from St Augustine's landing in England in AD 597 to the Crimean War in 1850.

Late in 1979 there will be a new exhibition on fossil man, and in 1980 an exhibition on plant reproduction and evolution.

The Natural History Museum's education services include a children's centre and a Natural History Club, which offers opportunities for seriously interested youngsters to take part in various activities. Public lectures are held regularly.

Practical details: Open Monday to Saturday from 10 am to 6 pm and on Sunday from 2.30 to 6 pm. Free admission. Nearest Underground station is South Kensington. Use buses 30, 39A, 45, 49 or 74. Refreshments available.

Address: Cromwell Road, South Kensington SW7 5BD. Telephone (01) 589 6323.

ORLEANS HOUSE

The Octagon

A riverside art gallery in Richmond

Orleans House, a stone's throw from the Thames, was built in 1710 by John James, a chief assistant to Sir Christopher Wren. The Octagon was added by James Gibbs ten years later. The Octagon, a most imposing structure, is 34 feet high and has a tall round-arched window on each of its three south-facing sides. Its style is similar to that of pavilions which were a feature of eighteenth-century German palace gardens.

The interior is domed and decorated in Roman baroque style, with stucco work by two distinguished specialists, Artari and Bagutti (who figured with Gibbs in the building of St Martin-in-the-Fields, London). There are medallions on the walls, probably portraying George II and Queen Caroline; a third could be Louis-Philippe, son of the Duke of Orleans and later King of France, who lived here from 1815 to 1817.

In 1926/27 most of Orleans House was demolished, but the remains, including the Octagon, were purchased by the Hon Mrs Ionides, who bequeathed the property and her collection of pictures of Richmond and Twickenham to the local authority in 1962. It is now a public art gallery, and shows a continuous programme of temporary exhibitions.

Practical details: Open Tuesday to Saturday from 1 to 5.30 pm, and on Sunday from 2 to 5.30 pm. Between October and March the closing time is 4.30 pm. The woodland garden is open daily from 9 am to sunset. Free admission. Nearest British Rail station is St Margaret's (SR) and the nearest Underground station is Richmond. Use buses 27, 33 or 90B.
Address: Riverside, Twickenham TW1 3DJ. Telephone (01) 940 0221.

NOTE: Ham House (see page 58) is across the river from Orleans House and can be reached by ferry in summer. Marble Hill House (see page 86) is adjacent to Orleans House, and on the same side of the river.

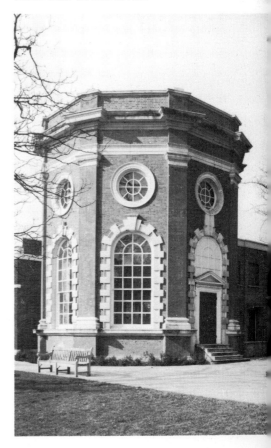

113

OSTERLEY PARK HOUSE

An Adam triumph

The splendours of an English country house

The Etruscan Dressing-Room.

Osterley was owned in its earlier days by the Childs, the famous banking family. An inventory of 1782 of the contents listed the furniture, and many of the rooms now appear as they were when Robert Adam, the great architect and interior designer, built and furnished them.

Seen from across the park, with a view of the great colonnade of the front porch, Osterley has an undoubted air of grandeur. Inside, Adam broke away from the heavy styles of other designers and concentrated on decorations which had no constructional purpose — he used delicate, graceful plaster mouldings on the walls and ceilings.

The Library has inset paintings by Zucchi and armchairs made by Linnell.

The Long Gallery, which sweeps across the full width of the house, is thought to have been the work of Sir William Chambers. It is hung with paintings, including Richard Wilson's *Landscape with Venus and Adonis,* for the most part lent by the Victoria & Albert Museum (which administers the house for the National Trust) to give an idea of its appearance in the late eighteenth century.

The Tapestry Room walls are entirely covered with tapestries. In the State Bedchamber is a lavishly ornamented and domed four-poster bed and a set of beautiful gilded armchairs, all designed by Adam. Adjoining is the Etruscan Dressing-Room, with an interesting and unusual décor, the designs on the walls and door panel having been copied by Adam from Greek vases and urns. It was not to everyone's liking. The author Horace Walpole, who visited Osterley from his home nearby, expressed the opinion that entering this room was like 'going out of a palace into a potter's field'!

Practical details: Open Tuesday to Sunday, April to September from 2 to 6 pm, and October to March from 12 noon to 4 pm. There is an admission charge. Nearby Underground stations are Osterley and Boston Manor. Use buses 111, 120 or E1, or Green Line coaches 704 or 705. Easy parking. Open spaces nearby. Refreshments available.

Address: Osterley, Middlesex TW7 4RB. Telephone (01) 560 3918.

OVERLORD EMBROIDERY

Tribute to D~Day

A latterday Bayeux Tapestry . . . unique memorial to the liberators of Europe

Lord Dulverton's tribute to the D-Day armies, the 272-feet-long Overlord Embroidery, is one of the most imaginative and beautiful of war memorials. Longer than the famous Bayeux Tapestry of Norman times, it was put on permanent display at Whitbread's Brewery in 1978 and unveiled in the 200-year-old Porter Tun Room by the Queen Mother. The Embroidery was designed by the Chelsea artist Sandra Lawrence, and it took 20 members of the Royal School of Needlework five years to work. The Embroidery's 34 panels, each eight feet long and three feet high, portray many aspects of Britain at war, with the accent on the D-Day invasion preparations and the Liberation of Europe.
The first few panels show Britain after the Dunkirk withdrawal, building up her forces, stimulating greater war production in the factories, and the Nazi air onslaught on British cities. The last few show bitter fighting in France, and Allied troops marching into the distance towards ultimate victory.
The Embroidery is based on authentic war references — photographs, drawings and documents — and is executed in appliqué. Much of the material it uses is genuine: for example, the uniforms shown on the panels employ fragments of real uniforms. Many faces familiar in wartime are instantly recognisable in the Embroidery: for example, General Eisenhower, King George VI, Field Marshal Montgomery and Winston Churchill.

Practical details: Open Monday to Saturday from 10 am to 5 pm and on Sunday from 2 to 6 pm. There is an admission charge. Nearest British Rail *and* Underground stations are Liverpool Street (ER) and Moorgate (ER). Nearest Underground stations are Old Street and Barbican. Use buses 11, 55, 76, 104, 133, 141, 214 or 271.
Address: Porter Tun Room, Whitbread's Brewery, Chiswell Street EC1Y 4SD. Telephone (01) 606 4455.

Monty and Churchill, in part of the massive 272-feet-long Overlord tapestry.

PERCIVAL DAVID FOUNDATION OF CHINESE ART

Chinese ceramics

Exquisite craftsmanship from the Sung, Yüan, Ming and Ch'ing dynasties

Only the connoisseur will appreciate the full subtleties of this collection of Chinese ceramics, but even visitors who lack specialized knowledge will recognize the beauty of the craftsmanship.

The collection numbers about 1,600 pieces dating from between the tenth and eighteenth centuries. Sir Percival David presented it to the University of London in 1951, with the object of stimulating interest in the art and culture of China and surrounding regions. In 1952 the collection was enlarged by the Elphinstone Gift of 171 monochrome works, principally from the eighteenth century.

Many of the porcelains were once owned by Chinese emperors, and several of them bear poems by Emperor Ch'ien Lung.

Practical details: Open on Monday from 2 to 5 pm, between Tuesday and Friday from 10.30 am to 5 pm, and on Saturday from 10.30 am to 1 pm. Free admission. Nearby British Rail stations are Euston (LMR), St Pancras and King's Cross (ER). Nearby Underground stations are Russell Square and Goodge Street. Use buses 14, 24, 29, 30, 68, 73, 77, 77A, 77C or 188.

Address: 53 Gordon Square WC1H 0PD. Telephone (01) 387 3909.

A 'birthday plate', said to have been made for the Emperor K'ang-hsi's sixtieth birthday in 1713.

POLLOCK'S TOY MUSEUM

Toy theatres

**Children's playthings from the past
— but still popular the world over**

Robert Louis Stevenson once wrote an
essay on toy theatres entitled *Penny
Plain, Twopence Coloured* after
visiting Pollock's shop. He was
referring to the play books, which
could be cut up into theatre parts,
characters and scenery, and were sold
complete with script. These were
popular in the early nineteenth
century — and have remained so.

Toy theatres are sold all over the world
from Pollock's, who have a museum
attached to their pleasingly old-
fashioned shop. The theatres are taken
from the original copperplate
engravings used by Mr Benjamin
Pollock and his predecessors. In the
museum is a tableau showing Mr
Green, one of the first toy theatre
publishers, working at his
copperplate press. Nearby a girl is
colouring sheets of scenery.

The museum's theatres occupy two
rooms. Fashioned from cardboard,
they are often quite elaborate. The
fronts of the theatres were authentic
copies of prosceniums in actual
nineteenth-century theatres, and the
players, also made of cardboard, were
often identified with well-known
actors of the time.

On show are two scenes from the most
popular play ever published, *The
Miller and His Men*, which was the
favourite of Winston Churchill, a
great toy-theatre enthusiast. The play
concludes with an explosion, which

probably accounts for its appeal. One of a number of English, French and Viennese toy theatres on exhibition is set for a play called *The Silver Palace.* It was used by the ballet impresario Diaghilev in the 1920s. There are two prosceniums dated 1820-30 — the earliest date ascribed to any of the theatres in this collection. One is showing *The Maid and the Magpie,* adapted from the Rossini opera, *The Thieving Magpie.*

Other rooms feature a wonderful range of toys from the Victorian era: wax dolls, carved animals, and street toys such as whip tops and hoops. There is also a display of optical toys, many of which depended for their effect on illusion. There are flick books and a Thaumatrope, a disc with a drawing on either side — for instance, of a bird and its cage, which when rotated with threads gives the impression that the bird was *in* the cage. The effect of moving pictures was obtained from another toy, the Zoetrope, by looking through slits in a circular frame at images on a rotating strip of drawings inside. The Praxinoscope, derived from this, employed an octagon of mirrors. Magic lanterns can be seen as well as an Urban Dioscope of 1898 — a forerunner of the cinematograph and one of the best projectors of its day.

Practical details: Open Monday to Saturday from 10 am to 5 pm. Toy theatre shows are held on Saturday, and there are special thematic exhibitions from time to time. There is an admission charge. Nearest Underground station is Goodge Street. Use buses 14, 24, 29, 73, 134 or 253.

Address: 1 Scala Street W1P 1LT. Telephone (01) 636 3452.

THE PUBLIC RECORD OFFICE

900 years of Government records

Domesday Book, Magna Carta, Guy Fawkes's confessions and dozens of royal autographs

The Public Record Office is a storehouse of most surviving documents of Government departments since the Norman Conquest. The bulk of these may be seen only by authorised ticket-holders — for example, by historians — but a number of the more significant documents of general interest are on permanent exhibition.

Domesday Book, which was ordered to be compiled by William the Conqueror in 1085, is the earliest and certainly the most celebrated exhibit on display in the museum.

There are two volumes, large and small, in the showcase and visitors can actually leaf through a facsimile version. Notice the archaic spellings of the counties: Lincolescire, Devenescire, Sudsexe and Chenth. Documents from the Middle Ages include Pipe Rolls — a record of tax collected by sheriffs, dating back to Henry I.

The intriguing story of the Gunpowder Plot of 1605 is spanned by four authentic papers: first, the anonymous letter to Lord Monteagle, warning him not to attend Parliament: 'They shall receyve a terrible blow this Parleament and yet

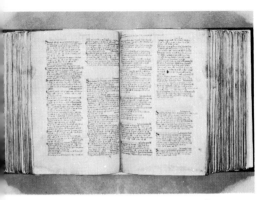

The original Domesday Book.

they shall not seie who hurts them.'
There is also a letter from James I
containing instructions for
questioning Guy Fawkes, and
suggesting torture if he did not
confess. Finally, there are two
confessions signed by Fawkes both
before and after torture in the Tower
of London.

There are many letters from royalty to
be seen: Catherine the Great, George I,
Louis XVI, Marie Antoinette, and a
version of Magna Carta — the
Inspeximus of Edward I (Edward's
'confirmation' of King John's
charter). of which two others are in the
Guildhall and one in Canberra.

Coming more up to date, there is an
interesting deciphered telephone
message from the British Embassy in
Moscow during World War I
describing the riots in Petrograd (now
Leningrad) which initiated the
Russian Revolution (1917).

The World War II period has provided
many historic exhibits: part of a letter
from Hitler to Neville Chamberlain,
the British premier, in 1939, and a
telegraphed report on the chances of
evacuating British troops from
Dunkirk: 'Given immunity from air
attack, troops could gradually be
evacuated provided food and boats can
be made available in sufficient
quantity.'

There are also a Battle of Britain
pilot's combat report, and a page from
the operations record book of No 617
Squadron on the successful Mohne
and Eder Dam raids. This squadron
figures, too, in a curious letter from
Air Marshal Arthur ('Bomber') Harris,
who reiterated a suggestion turned
down earlier that British bombers
should make simultaneous raids on
Mussolini's home and office. He
wanted No 617 Squadron for the job.
The idea was never followed up.

Forty royal autographed documents
are on show: a letter signed by the
Black Prince in 1370; another by Anne
Boleyn dated 1529; and a touching
letter from Catherine Howard to her
ill-fated lover Thomas Culpeper, who
was later hanged for adultery. George
VI's consent to the marriage of the
present Queen is there, sealed with the
Great Seal. The Coronation Oath,
signed by the Queen, is the most recent
royal autograph.

Various curiosities also find a place
here: the indictment of Dick Turpin
for stealing a black mare and a foal in
Yorkshire in 1739, for which he was
found guilty and hanged; and the
report by Lieutenant Bligh on the
mutiny on the *Bounty*.

Practical details: Open Monday to
Friday from 1 to 4 pm. Conducted
parties by arrangement with the
Keeper, on (01) 405 3488 extension 475.
Free admission. Nearest Underground
station is Chancery Lane. Use buses 6,
9, 9A, 11 or 15.

Address: Chancery Lane WC2A 1LR.
Telephone (01) 405 0741 — with
general enquiries.

RAF MUSEUM

Warriors of the air

From the Blériot to the mighty Lancaster bomber and the high-speed jet fighters . . . and a tribute to 'The Few'

'No enemy plane shall fly over the Reich territory,' boasted Nazi air force chief Hermann Goering. Just how wrong he was can be seen from the markings on the mighty Avro Lancaster four-engined bomber which dominates the 40 aircraft displayed under one roof at Hendon. Symbol of our air offensive in World War II, this 'Lanc' survived 137 operational sorties'.

The RAF Museum, situated on the old Hendon airfield, was opened by the Queen in 1972. It is exceptionally well laid-out.

The Aircraft Hall, the main feature, is housed in one of the old airfield's original hangars, so arranged that in a short stroll the visitor can span the whole history of aircraft. These begin

with a Bleriot monoplane, as used for Blériot's historic Channel crossing in 1909, then through both world wars and into the 1970s. A collection of aircraft in the centre of the hall honours designer Sir Sydney Camm, for many years with the Hawker company.

Man took to the air before the invention of powered flight, and there are many relics of the balloon age, including a basket used by the Royal Engineers' Balloon Battalion, founded in the 1870s, and the curious man-lifting kite invented by Colonel S F Cody.

There are scale models of aircraft by the score, many of them figuring in dioramas. One shows an attack on shell-battered trenches in World War I, another a World War II fighter station. The museum abounds with relics of men and machines, armaments, components, flying aids and other examples of technological advance in aviation, both civil and military.

Tableaux with life-size figures include a Royal Flying Corps and Royal Naval Air Service workshop, and a messroom of the Women's Royal Air Force in 1918. An interesting piece of history from World War II is the Battle of Britain signature board from the White Hart public house near Biggin Hill, the famous fighter station in Kent. The names of aces chalked here include 'Sailor' Malan, Johnny Johnson and Neville Duke.

Lord Trenchard, that great leader of the RAF, has a gallery devoted largely to himself, with insignia and decorations, including his Order of Merit and his mantle as a Knight

Lord Trenchard, Marshal of the RAF.

120

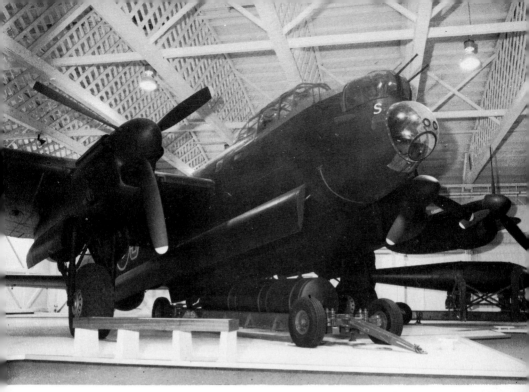

Grand Cross of the Order of the Bath. Trenchard served under half a dozen monarchs, and one case shows the uniforms of three of them: George V, Edward VIII and George VI (whose decorations are also on display). Many aviation pioneers and personalities are commemorated in the art gallery. Exhibits demonstrate Sir Barnes Wallis's famous 'bouncing bomb' — the one used to devastate the Mohne and Eder dams, as shown in the celebrated film *The Dambusters*. With the introduction of high-speed jet aircraft late in World War II, baling out became a sometimes fatal experience for fighter pilots. Sir James Martin's answer to this was the ejection seat, which blasts a pilot from his cockpit and allows him to descend by parachute. On show is a Martin-Baker ejection seat — a device which has saved more than 4,000 lives. On weekdays, free film shows are

Avro Lancaster, at the RAF Museum.

---

given at the museum.

BATTLE OF BRITAIN MUSEUM

The Battle of Britain Museum, which forms part of the RAF Museum complex, was opened by the Queen Mother in November 1978 as a national tribute to Britain's wartime forces and especially to 'The Few' who actually fought the Battle of Britain. The biggest exhibit is a Coastal Command four-engined Short Sunderland — the only complete one left in the country — which is exhibited alongside the famous Westland Lysander. Other British aircraft include Spitfire, Hurricane, Blenheim, Defiant and Gladiator (the RAF's last biplane fighter), as well as several German planes; for example, two Messerschmitts, a Junkers and a Heinkel 111.

121

In the centre of the museum is a continuous slide show which describes in pictures how and why the Battle of Britain was fought, and impressive photographs of the 'Blitz' on London and other cities that followed — the Germans' attempt to demoralise civilians. There are several life-sized tableaux. One shows a typical air-raid incident with ARP workers and civilians amid the rubble; and there are exhibits portraying an Observer Corps post, barrage balloon and searchlight units.

Upstairs visitors can look down on an impressive full-sized replica of the Operations Room of No 11 Group, Fighter Command. This was actually at Uxbridge during the war and controlled fighter squadrons defending the much-attacked southeast of England. It is complete with personnel, and panels on the wall show the state of the squadrons as at 11.30 am on September 15th, 1940 — the day that the Prime Minister, Mr Winston Churchill, visited the headquarters.

Also upstairs are many photographs, and the RAF uniforms of King George VI and Lord Dowding, chief of Fighter Command.

Practical details: Open Monday to Saturday from 10 am to 6 pm and on Sunday from 2 to 6 pm. Admission to the main RAF Museum is free, but there is a charge to visit the Battle of Britain Museum. Nearest Underground station is Colindale. Use buses 32, 79, 113, 251, 266 or 292. Easy parking. Refreshments available.

Address: Aerodrome Road, Hendon NY4 4SS. Telephone (01) 205 2266.

RANGER'S HOUSE

Elizabethan and Jacobean portraits

A fine seventeenth-century brick villa, on the edge of Greenwich Park

Ranger's House was begun in 1688 by Andrew Snape, the King's Serjeant-Farrier, and was later occupied by the 4th Earl of Chesterfield, the statesman and author. In 1902 it was bought by the London County Council. It is now an art gallery housing the Suffolk Collection of paintings.

The collection's principal attraction is an impressive series of Elizabethan and Jacobean full-length portraits, all magnificently costumed. They include an English ambassador to Moscow in 1585, Sir Jerome Bowes; other noblemen and their wives, and some ladies of the Court. Lely, Kneller and Wissing have paintings here — including those of Charles II, James II and their wives and mistresses.

Practical details: Open daily, including Sunday, from 10 am to 5 pm. From November to January the closing time is 4 pm. Free admission. Nearby British Rail stations are Blackheath (SR) and Greenwich (SR). Use buses 53, 54 or 75. There are river launches to Greenwich from Westminster and Charing Cross piers. Easy parking. Open spaces nearby.

Address: Chesterfield Walk, Blackheath SE10. Telephone (01) 853 0035.

ROYAL BOTANIC GARDENS (KEW GARDENS)

Colour by the acre

The nation's huge historic garden that have not only beauty but scientific purpose

The great Palm House at Kew.

Ranged along the foot of the great Palm House Terrace overlooking the pond in Kew Gardens are stone replicas of ten heraldic beasts. They were sculpted by James Woodford from his plaster originals which stood outside the Westminster Abbey Annexe during the Coronation of Queen Elizabeth II in 1953.

These statues symbolize Kew's strong connection with royalty. It was Princess Augusta, the mother of George III, who started the gardens — in a private capacity — in 1759 with her nine-acre botanical garden. Her house is no longer there, but the Orangery near which it stood, the work of Sir William Chambers, the Princess's architect, is still in handsome shape.

Kew Gardens, while a splendid living museum of trees, fruit and flowers, has always been above all a scientific establishment. It identifies plants, conducts research into them and acts as a distribution centre for plants, both decorative and economic. It is thanks to Kew, and its efforts to introduce plants from one part of the world to others, that South-East Asia, principally Malaya, has established a rubber industry.

The living collections total about 45,000 plant species, and it is these that most visitors go to see. The colourful face of Kew changes with the seasons, for there are many 'special areas' devoted to one species of plant. The Rhododendron Dell, planted out more than a hundred years ago, is resplendent from the middle of May to early June. Others are the Rock and Aquatic Gardens, with places for heaths, roses, a lily pond, and beds comprising the Herbaceous Ground. Kew has a range of glasshouses, many of them heated for the cultivation of tropical or sub-tropical plants. In House No 10 is the great Amazon Water Lily, which can grow from a seed to a plant with leaves six feet in diameter in seven months.

A major landmark at Kew is the Palm House, 360 feet long, planned by Decimus Burton (who also designed the cast iron main gate) and erected in the 1840s. This contains plants from the tropics. Palms are naturally prominent, but there are also bananas, bamboos and other economic plants, including the sources of drugs, resins, rubber and gutta-percha. The temperature here is maintained at 50-

123

60 degrees Fahrenheit in winter, and 70-80 degrees in summer.

Kew is rich in large-scale 'garden ornaments'. The most prominent is the 163-feet-high Pagoda, designed by Sir William Chambers in 1761 purely as a decorative feature. Three temples dotted around the gardens were also designed by Sir William; a fourth is King William's Temple, near the Temperate House, and was built much later, in 1837. The towering flagstaff is a Douglas fir 225 feet high and about 370 years old. It was given by the Government of British Columbia.

There is also a replica of a famous Japanese gate, 'Chokushi Mon', which was featured at the Japanese-British Exhibition at Shepherd's Bush in 1910. Also from the East are the impressive pair of Chinese Guardian Lions, which overlook the pond.

The Dutch House, known as Kew Palace, was built in 1631 and was acquired by King George III 150 years later. The King, known as 'Farmer George' because of his enthusiasm for country living, enjoyed his frequent spells in rural Kew. The Palace is open in summer and is worth seeing for its period furniture and paintings.

In the Marianne North Gallery, near the east wall of Kew Gardens, is a remarkable collection of 848 oil paintings of flowers. Miss North painted them all between 1872 and 1885, and visited many parts of the world for her subjects.

Kew Gardens has three museums which are open to the public. The Wood Museum has a prolific range of plank specimens from all over the world, particularly the Commonwealth. There is a cross-section of a giant sequoia tree, 16 feet in diameter and more than 1,300 years old; and a scene in cork of a town in Freiburg. In the upper gallery are shown the many different uses of wood.

The General Museum gives visitors a detailed insight into plants and their life, cultivation and uses. Displays show how rubber and tobacco are produced, the sources of edible oils and the many uses of medicinal plants.

The Orangery illustrates the value and extent of Kew's work as a unique scientific institution.

Several buildings are open only for research or study. The Herbarium, a building block to the right of the main gates, was founded in 1852, and contains what is thought to be the largest collection of botanical material in the world: between four and five million mounted sheets of specimens, over 35,000 glass jars of flowers and fruit in preservative, and a reference collection of seeds.

There are two laboratories, and a library which includes some 100,000 volumes, 140,000 reprints, and an illustrations collection of more than 160,000 flower paintings, engravings and photographs.

Practical details: Open daily from 10 am, closing between 4 and 7 pm, depending on the season. Glasshouses open at 11 am and close not later than 4.50 pm on weekdays and 5.50 pm on Sundays. The admission charge is 1p. Nearest British Rail station is Kew Bridge (SR), and the nearest Underground station is Kew Gardens. Use buses 27, 65, 117, 203, 237, 267, E1 or E2. Easy parking. Open spaces. Refreshments available.

Address: Kew, Richmond, Surrey TW9 3AB. Telephone (01) 940 1171.

Early musical instruments

A 500-year-old harpsichord, Haydn's clavichord, and the 'deep-voiced' contrabassophon are in this mecca for musicians

From this richly diverse collection of nearly 500 instruments, the clavicytherium rates as the earliest stringed keyboard in the world. This instrument, the earliest type of upright harpsichord, has been dated *c* 1480. It was once owned by Count Correr of Venice, and eventually it found its way into the Donaldson Collection, one of five large collections which have swollen the museum's own stock of ancient instruments over the past 90 years. The clavicytherium, frail and damaged by woodworm, has been copied by Adlam Burnett, and the replica was played in public for the first time in 1973, with delightful results.

The College collection includes many other precious keyboard instruments: an Italian harpsichord of 1580, and a virginal, made by Celestini of Venice in 1593, beautifully decorated with

miniatures. Even older is a harpsichord by Alessandro Trasuntino dated 1531. An interesting link with Haydn is his clavichord (made by Joann Bohak) dated 1794. There is a chamber organ of 1702, made by Bernard Smith of London, which was formerly at Brick Wall,

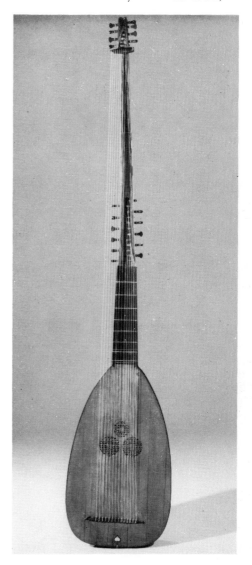

A Chitarrone, one of the many rare instruments at the Royal College of Music.

Sussex, then for 30 years at Winchester College.

The wind instruments include recorders, flutes, oboes, clarinets, bassoons, serpents and some nineteenth-century brass.

A rare instrument on view is the contrabassophon — a type of contra-bassoon — which has a note louder and deeper than any other woodwind.

The stringed instruments include viols, lutes and citterns as well as a selection of seventeenth-century guitars, decorated in tortoise-shell and ivory. There are a number of hurdy-gurdies, inlaid with mother-of-pearl and ivory, ranging in date from the sixteenth to eighteenth centuries. Also harps, psalteries and dulcimers.

The museum also has an ethnological collection of instruments from China, Japan, India, the Middle and Near East and Africa.

The Royal College of Music's Department of Portraits possesses a gallery of 120 paintings and 3,000 engravings and photographs — all portraits of musicians — which is open to view. In the same department is a collection of concert programmes and other musical ephemera.

Practical details: The museum is open on Monday and Wednesday during term time, from 10.30 am to 4.30 pm, by appointment with the Curator. There is an admission charge. The Department of Portraits is open Monday to Friday during term time, from 10 am to 5 pm, by appointment with the Keeper of Portraits. Free admission. Nearest Underground station is South Kensington. Use buses 9, 52 or 73.

Address: Prince Consort Road, South Kensington SW7 2BS. Telephone (01) 589 3643.

ROYAL HOSPITAL MUSEUM

Soldiers in retirement

Relics of battles, long since fought and won, on view in fine buildings designed by Sir Christopher Wren

The old soldiers who 'never die' but 'only fade away' — the Chelsea Pensioners — live in this hospital, which was founded by Charles II in 1682. The secretary's office and museum building in East Road was built by Sir John Soane in 1819. The museum is very conscious of the first Duke of Wellington's role in military history. A large picture of the Battle of Waterloo by George Jones, RA, dominates the secretary's office hall, and a key chart to the leading figures rests on a long table — the one which bore the Duke's coffin when it lay in state in the Hospital's Great Hall. Original plans and maps of the Hospital are displayed in the

The home of the famous Chelsea Pensioners.

museum, with many photographs of royal occasions. Trophies include a dervish flag captured at Omdurman. The Pensioners formerly carried arms, and a cluster of these is on show: halberds, muskets and bayonets.

There are also a Bible and Prayer Book which were given by Florence Nightingale in the Crimea to a soldier who later became a Pensioner.

In the Medal Room there are 1,700 medals which once belonged to Pensioners. The campaigns in which they took part go back to Waterloo, for which the earliest English medals were awarded — the first campaign medals ever struck by the Government.

The Chapel here was completed by Wren in 1687. Its wainscoting and pews are mainly original, and the silver-gilt altar plate — including alms dish, candlesticks, flagons and chalices — are hallmarked 1687-8. Parade services, which visitors are welcome to attend, are held here on Sunday mornings.

The Great Hall, on the opposite side of the passage, is used as a dining-hall — its original purpose. The mural shows Charles II on horseback with the Royal Hospital in the background: it was begun by Verrio and completed by Henry Cooke.

Practical details: The Main Hospital grounds are open on weekdays from 10 am to 12 noon and from 2 to 6 pm. Also on Sunday from 2 to 6 pm. The museum, Chapel and Great Hall are open at the same times, except that they close at 4 pm. Free admission. Nearest Underground station is Sloane Square. Use buses 11 or 137. **Address:** Royal Hospital Road, SW3 4SL. Telephone (01) 730 0161 extension 46.

THE ROYAL MEWS

All the Queen's horses...

... And all her coaches and landaus too, with a right royal show of harness

Much of the colour and splendour of royal occasions begins in the Royal Mews, a quadrangle of stables and coach-houses in the grounds of Buckingham Palace. Here are kept a variety of coaches and landaus and the horses that draw them, as well as the Queen's small fleet of cars.

The present Mews succeeded the previous stables, maintained in Trafalgar Square and Bloomsbury from the time of Richard II, and were built in 1825 to John Nash's design. At one time they were in the charge of the Master of the Horse. The officer now responsible is the Crown Equerry, though the Master of the Horse (since 1978, the Earl of Westmorland) still fulfils his role as the third great officer of the Court and functions as senior personal attendant to the Queen on all occasions which involve the use of horses.

The first coach to be seen in the Mews is the Gold State Coach, associated above all with coronations. In this reign it has been used for the Coronation in 1953 and for the Thanksgiving Service at St Paul's Cathedral on the occasion of the Silver Jubilee in 1977.

Gilded wooden carvings of tritons, cherubs, dolphins, shells, palm trees and other ornamentation contribute to the elaborate coachwork decoration, which includes of course the symbolic paintings on the panelling, the work of the Italian historical painter Cipriani. The coach weighs four tons and takes eight postillion horses to draw it at walking pace.

In the Coach Houses there are small vehicles — clarences, broughams, phaetons and victorias — many of considerable historic interest. Some were built for Queen Victoria. There is also a donkey barouche, pulled by a Shetland pony and used at Windsor by the royal children.

In the State Carriage House is a glittering collection of coaches. Probably the most famous of these is the Glass Coach, so named because of its large windows, and used for royal weddings, including those of the present Queen, Princess Anne and Princess Alexandra. The Irish State Coach, usually used by the Queen for the State Opening of Parliament, is beautifully designed in black with abundant gold trimmings, and surmounted by a crown.

Queen Alexandra's State Coach was used by the Queen for Princess Margaret's wedding, and it conveys foreign ambassadors to the Palace to present their credentials on appointment. The Queen meets foreign heads of state in the 1902 State Postillion landau, first used by Edward VII for his first state drive to the City of London. There are several state landaus to be seen: these are lighter than the coaches and are frequently used as open carriages on ceremonial occasions.

The horses used for the Queen's carriage are always greys, and for the other royal carriages either greys or bays, though the chosen types have changed over the years; at various periods in history, cream horses and blacks have also been in vogue. The horses can be seen by the public, though in late summer many of them are out to grass in the country.

In the State Harness Room are the often highly-ornamented sets of leather and brass-mounted harness (the No 1 set, used with the State Coach, is gilt). Many are historic: for example, the two sets of Blue State Harness, made in 1791. Also displayed are the various liveries used by coachmen and postillions for state, semi-state or ordinary occasions.

Many more historic items can be seen in the Saddlery next door: the saddles used by Queen Victoria and Queen Alexandra, riding whips presented to reigning monarchs, saddle cloths. Among the gifts of saddles is a Russian one presented by Mr Bulganin and Mr Khrushchev on their 1957 visit to England. Among the oldest on show is the highly decorated one which belonged to George IV. A special exhibit which should not be missed is the saddlery used by the Queen for the Trooping the Colour ceremony.

Finally, in the Old Carriage House, are a dozen sleighs and small carts, including a 'State Sledge' used by Queen Victoria and made to Prince Albert's design.

Practical details: Open on Wednesday and Thursday only, from 2 to 4 pm. Closed during Royal Ascot race meeting in June. There is an admission charge. Nearest British Rail *and* Underground station is Victoria (SR). Use buses 11, 16, 38, 52 or 507.

Address: Buckingham Palace SW1A 1AA.

ST BRIDE'S
CRYPT MUSEUM

The journalists' church

Links with Caxton, and visible remains of Roman, Saxon and Norman buildings beneath a fine Wren church

In the year 1500, Wynkyn de Worde, one of William Caxton's assistants, brought Caxton's printing press from Westminster to a site next to the churchyard of St Bride's: unwittingly, he was helping to establish Fleet Street as the great centre of the printed word.

The church, the eighth on the site, was rebuilt in 1675 by Sir Christopher Wren. Recently, thanks to Sir Max Aitken, when proprietor of the Beaverbrook Press, the crypt has been converted into a museum as well as a chapel. St Bride's now houses a fine facsimile of Caxton's translation of Ovid's *Metamorphoses*, of 1480.

St Bride's has at least twice been gutted by fire: once in the Great Fire of 1666, and again when the rebuilt church was all but destroyed by German bombs in 1940. One interesting survival in the church is the font of 1615 in which Samuel Pepys was baptized.

In the crypt the museum's first exhibit is a facsimile of an evening newspaper's front page, dated 30th December 1940, showing the church's devastation. As if in part compensation for the war damage, the bombing havoc revealed what are now the museum's biggest exhibits — church walls built in the sixth, nineth, twelfth, fifteenth and seventeenth centuries and still *in situ*. Also noteworthy are an iron coffin of 1818, flanged and with spring-clips so as to be secure from body-snatchers; a fragment of a Saxon font; Norman masonry; remains of a second-century Roman pavement and the line of a first century Roman ditch; and a stone tomb dating from Norman times.

Copies of pages from ancient newspapers and books proliferate, along with old maps of the area and documents relating to the Great Plague: there were three major plague pits in the parish. On display is a first edition of *Pamela* by Samuel Richardson, commonly regarded as the first English novel, published in 1741. There is a Breeches Bible (dated 1560), so-called because of its description of the first clothing of Adam and Eve in Genesis iii, 7: 'They sewed figge tree leaves together and made themselves Breeches.'

Near the museum's entrance are a brown silk party-dress and part of a hand-embroidered wedding dress. They belonged to Susannah, wife of William Rich, a baker whose shop was on Ludgate Hill. One of his specialities was a wedding cake modelled on St Bride's famous steeple.

Practical details: Open daily from 9 am to 5 pm. Free admission, though contributions towards maintenance costs are welcome. Nearest Underground station is Blackfriars. Use buses 4, 6, 9, 9A, 11, 15, 45, 46, 63 or 171.

Address: Fleet Street EC4Y 8AU. Telephone (01) 353 1301.

ST JOHN'S GATE AND MUSEUM

The first crusaders

Step back 800 years in this ancient headquarters . . . and see ancient relics of the Knights of St John

The ancient embattled gate spanning the narrow St John's Lane was once the main entrance of the Priory of Clerkenwell of the Order of St John and dates back to the twelfth century. It now houses the headquarters of the

Most Venerable Order of the Hospital of St John of Jerusalem, the British Order, which has worldwide connections. It was revived in the last century after a lapse of 300 years. The original order was founded in the twelfth century.

Today, the work of the British Order is channelled through St John Ambulance and an ophthalmic hospital in Jerusalem.

Rebuilt in Tudor times, with some Jacobean additions, the Gate has two four-storey towers, with the large Council Chamber spanning the archway across the road. The rooms themselves being largely unaltered, the ancient atmosphere is preserved.

All round the walls of the Chapter Hall (a 1903 extension, in Tudor style) are the painted shields of all the Priors of the Priory of England.

In the museum, one of the most important exhibits is the *Rhodes Missal,* a beautifully illuminated prayer book. It was presented to the Order in Rhodes in 1504 by a French Grand Prior, and contains 28 miniatures illustrating Bible history.

There are several other sixteenth-century books and documents, as well as the original manuscript, signed by Henry VIII, of the warrant to destroy the priory church in Clerkenwell in 1546. (Difficulties with Rome had forced Henry to dissolve the Order of St John in England six years earlier.) The earliest illustrated book on the Order is the Ulm edition of Caoursain's *Obsidionis Rhodiae* of 1496, which contains 36 woodcuts.

The museum contains coinage of the order, pieces of Maltese silver and a Spanish parcel gilt chalice, reputedly brought here by Philip of Spain when he came to marry Queen Mary.

Particularly impressive is a finely-worked silver sixteenth-century cross, probably French, which is still carried on ceremonial occasions.

Centuries ago the Knights of St John often found themselves involved in defensive wars, and there are examples of arms and armour used by them and their forces at Rhodes and Malta. There is shot thought to have been used at the Siege of Rhodes in 1522, and a cannon — one of 19 given by Henry VIII in 1527 to help with the proposed recapture of Rhodes.

Other historic exhibits include three tattered banners, all captured by Napoleon in Malta in 1798.

The St John Ambulance Brigade is the subject of a special permanent exhibition. It includes early uniforms, awards and relics, such as a surgeon's tourniquet from the Crimean War.

The nearby Priory Church was first dedicated in 1185, but was burnt down during the Peasants' Revolt of 1381 and rebuilt in the fifteenth century. The nave is hung with banners of the Order. In the crypt there is a fine alabaster tomb sculpture of a Spanish Knight of the Order.

Practical details: The museum is open on Tuesday, Friday and Saturday from 10 am to 6 pm. There are conducted tours of the Grand Priory Church and St John's Gate at 11 am and 2.30 pm on these days. Large parties and special tours can be accommodated on other weekdays by arrangement. Free admission, though contributions are welcome. Nearby Underground stations are Farringdon and Barbican. Use buses 4, 5, 55, 63, 168, 243, 277 or 279.

Address: St John's Lane, Clerkenwell EC1M 4DA. Telephone (01) 253 6644.

One of the huge bronze cannons given to the Knights of St John by Henry VIII in 1522 to help with the proposed re-capture of Rhodes.

SALISBURY HALL AND MOSQUITO MUSEUM

The day of the Mosquito

Where Nell Gwyn and Winston Churchill lived . . . and the famous Mosquito aircraft was born

Salisbury Hall is not a museum, but a seventeenth-century manor house, privately owned by artist Mr Walter Goldsmith, which is open to view. Besides being beautifully furnished to match its period, the house has many historic associations. In a house on this site lived Asgar the Staller in AD 800 and Sir Richard Neville, the Earl of Warwick.

Nell Gwyn lived in a cottage next to the moat. Here, it is said, she persuaded Charles II to give a title to one of their three illegimate children by rushing to the window and holding the child over a 30-foot drop until the horrified king shouted: 'Spare the Duke of St Albans!'.

Winston Churchill stayed here with his mother, Lady Randolph Churchill, when she lived here in 1905. Later, this was the home of Sir Nigel Gresley, the locomotive designer, and a model of the record-breaking Pacific streamlined engine *Mallard,* is on show in the Hall.

The most recent role of this delightful moated house came shortly before the outbreak of World War II. It was requisitioned as a design centre for a new revolutionary type of fast bomber made of *wood.* In a hastily constructed hangar in the grounds, the full-sized plywood and paper mock-up of the twin-engined De Havilland Mosquito took shape, and the first prototype, W4050. You can see it today, resplendent in its yellow livery, 30 yards from where it was first made. A recorded commentary by Group Captain John Cunningham accompanies the exhibition.

The De Havilland Mosquito, probably the most versatile aircraft of World War II.

More than 7,000 of them were produced, to be employed on photo-reconnaissance, mine-laying, torpedo dropping, as courier, day and night fighter and submarine killer. It was capable of carrying a 4,000-pound 'blockbuster' bomb.

Precision bombing was among its duties. One notable sortie was the attack on Amiens jail to free 200 imprisoned members of the French Resistance under sentence of death.

Mosquitos were also widely used by Air Vice-Marshal Donald Bennett's Pathfinder Force, which illuminated targets for Allied bomber forces over Germany.

Many items of aviation interest can be seen alongside the Mosquito prototype, including 1,000 model aircraft spanning the history of flight. Two jet aircraft, a Vampire and Venom, are on display near the hangar.

All proceeds of the exhibition (less maintenance costs) are donated to the RAF Benevolent Fund and other charities.

Practical details: The house and museum are open only between Easter and the end of September, on Sunday from 2 to 6 pm. From July to September they are also open on Thursday afternoon. Bank Holiday opening times are from 10.30 am to 12.30 pm and 2 to 5.30 pm. There are admission charges to both the house and garden, and the Mosquito exhibition. Nearest British Rail station is St Albans (ER). Use buses 84 or 313, or Green Line coaches 707, 717, 724 or 727. Easy parking. Open spaces nearby. Refreshments available.

Address: On the A6, near London Colney, Hertfordshire AL2 1BU. Telephone Bowmans Green 23274.

SALVATION ARMY MUSEUM

Blood and fire

Parading with the Army was once a crime . . . A great movement remembers its early days

'Some men's ambition is art;
Some men's ambition is fame;
Some men's ambition is gold;
My ambition is the souls of men.'

These words were written in the autograph album of King Edward VII by General William Booth, founder and first Commander-in-Chief of The Salvation Army, in 1904. They are the signpost which pointed General Booth along his way of life, and many of the milestones on the route are to be seen in this small but informative museum.

William Booth began as a Methodist minister, but withdrew from the ministry to form The Christian Mission in 1865, which became The Salvation Army (motto: 'Blood and Fire') in 1878. The communion vessels he used as a minister are on display, and so is the uniform of the Army's first captain, ex-chimney sweep Elijah Cadman, his cap, bugle, drumsticks, long-service medal and photograph. In the early days of the Army, its members were regarded as a public

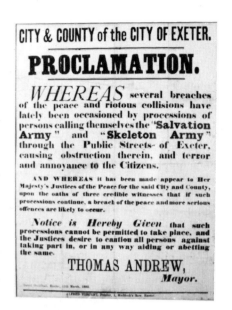

A proclamation in Exeter, banning processions of the newly formed 'Salvation Army' because of the 'riotous collisions' which were filling the gaols.

nuisance; cuttings from contemporary newspapers seen here describe efforts to stamp out their parades. In 1882, we are told, no fewer than 669 Salvationists were physically assaulted; two years later, 600 of them were in prison. A telegram to General Booth from an officer reports a 'terrible riot' in Bridgwater, and this is also on show.

One showcase illustrates the evolution of the women Salvationists' famous bonnet, modified nine times over the years, but nevertheless still a bonnet, and a distinctive feature of the uniform to this day. Nearby is a broad-arrowed convict's uniform — the very one worn by journalist W T Stead when imprisoned while working with

Booth to achieve the raising of the age of consent in order to protect young girls. Stead was sentenced to three months' imprisonment for experimentally obtaining a child who was handed over to The Salvation Army.

Salvationists have always prided themselves on practising what they preach: hence the relief of poverty in Victorian times through the establishment of hostels and factories, and 'farthing breakfasts', all over the country. Also the Hadleigh Colony, with its farm, hostel, shelter and brickworks, in Essex. Old photographs show these in operation, along with the people who had cause to be grateful to them.

General Booth himself received thanks, congratulations and good wishes from many parts of Britain and the world, to which a book of illuminated addresses bears witness. (Today the Army is at work in 81 countries.) There are also the casket and scroll presented to his son and successor, General Bramwell Booth, on being given the Freedom of Halifax in 1925.

Other exhibits include musical instruments and photographs of early bandsmen, and a recording of General Booth's voice reading from his address, 'More Rope Wanted'.

Practical details: Open Monday to Friday from 10 am to 12 noon and from 1 to 4 pm. Also open on Sunday from 10 am to 12 noon. Free admission, though contributions are welcome. Nearest British Rail *and* Underground station is King's Cross (ER). Use buses 14, 18, 30, 46, 73, 214 or 221. Refreshments available.

Address: Judd Street, King's Cross WC1H 9NN. Telephone (01) 387 1656.

THE SCIENCE MUSEUM

Knowledge is power

From space capsule to impulse generator and ancient railway locomotive . . . how man has harnessed natural forces

Fortunately for posterity, many men have a sense of history as well as a knowledge of science, and so many of the tools, instruments and work of the pioneer scientists and engineers have been preserved. In fact, there is so much to see in this, the national museum of science and technology, that one expert has estimated it would take two years to look round it all carefully.

Among the various early engines in the motive power section are survivors from the Industrial Revolution. One is the rotative engine that James Watt made with his partner Matthew Boulton for driving mill machinery. Inside the museum's main entrance is the 79-foot-long Foucault Pendulum. Although a pendulum always tends to swing in the same direction, this one appears to vary by about one degree of arc in five minutes. However, it is not the pendulum that has shifted, but the earth rotating beneath it. Another working model is the million-volt impulse generator, which is demonstrated twice a day with a crack loud enough to be heard almost throughout the museum.

Not far away stands 'Puffing Billy', the oldest railway locomotive in existence (dated 1813). Both the

Deep sea diving suit at the Science Museum: a museum to delight every young person.

genuine Stephenson's 'Rocket' (1829) and a replica, cut away to show its workings, are exhibited. They make an interesting contrast with the twentieth-century steam locomotive 'Caerphilly Castle', and the London Underground car which ran on the Piccadilly Line from 1929 to 1961. In the transport section there are also early motor-cars, motor-cycles, bicycles and fire-engines.

The actual Apollo 10 command module used in 1969 as the 'dress rehearsal' for the landing on the Moon.

Also on the ground floor is an exhibition called 'Exploration', which shows how modern man is using his scientific and technical skills to investigate his world. This covers underwater exploration, manned spaceflight, the planets and beyond, medical science, remote sensing and climatology. Among the large and spectacular items here is the actual command module used by three astronauts to splash down after the Apollo 10 mission in 1969 — a 'dress rehearsal' for the Apollo 11 landing on the moon. A huge, life-size tableau of

the Apollo 11 moon landing shows Neil Armstrong and Buzz Aldrin exploring the realistic moonscape. A daily talk on astronomy, and a demonstration, are given in the Star Dome on the first floor. Many historic astronomical instruments can be seen here, including the 7-foot-long, wood-encased reflecting telescope used by William Herschel, discoverer of the planet Uranus in 1781.
Nearby is a pump which takes in London air from the museum roof to measure air pollution. The results — filter-papers bearing grey smudges — are on display week by week.
The famous Wells Cathedral Clock (dated 1392) is on this floor. It is one of the two oldest surviving clocks in England, and has an elaborate

chiming mechanism. It has puzzled scientists how such sophisticated devices as these developed out of the blue in an unmechanical age.

On this floor too is a gallery on the modern gas industry. It describes in models, audio-visual demonstrations and realistic reconstructions what has become one of Britain's most progressive industries: one concentrating on the distribution of energy.

The Iron and Steel Gallery on this floor is in two sections. One shows the development of iron and steel-making up to the turn of the century, and the other describes up-to-date methods.

The second-floor galleries are devoted to navigation, shipping, mathematics and computing, pure and industrial chemistry, and printing and papermaking. 'Computing then and now' includes early computers and differential analysers (one is made of Meccano!), and a computer terminal which can be operated by visitors.

Printing and papermaking is the first collection to be displayed in the museum's new 'infill' block. It aims to show the development of the printing and papermaking industries from their earliest beginnings to the advanced technology of today. Many of the exhibits are operational, and demonstrations of some of the printing equipment and of hand papermaking can be arranged for parties by prior request. One of the exhibits is a lifesize tableau of an early nineteenth-century printing shop.

Here, too, is the Wilson Cloud Chamber, invented by C T R Wilson in 1912 to make visible tracks of ionising particles emitted by radio-active substances. The button-operated exhibit shows alpha particles darting out from plutonium. An animated diagram nearby explains the chain reaction in an atomic pile, and a small model shows Cockroft's and Walton's room at Cavendish Laboratory, Cambridge, where they split the atom in 1932.

Original equipment used in Marconi's early wireless experiments, and some Baird television apparatus, are featured on the third floor, where a large gallery is devoted to telecommunications.

There are more than 20 full-sized aircraft in the aeronautics sections, including a full-size reproduction of the Wright 'Flyer', in which the Wright Brothers achieved sustained powered flight for the first time, in 1903. There is also the Vickers Vimy aircraft in which Alcock and Brown made their momentous transatlantic crossing by air in 1919.

The development of the turbo-jet engine by Frank Whittle at once improved aircraft speeds and efficiency, and the W1 engine which powered the first jet flight in England in 1941 is on view, with the plane itself. Also to be seen is the 'Flying Bedstead', the experimental vertical take-off rig — a descendant of which is the 'Harrier' jump jet.

The strange-looking metal 'bubble' at the edge of the aeronautical section is Professor Piccard's stratosphere gondola, in which he made a 12-hour balloon flight in 1932. He ascended 10½ miles in order to study cosmic radiation, and suffered temperatures down to minus 60 degrees Centigrade.

There are many models of rockets here, including the 2,700-ton Apollo-Saturn rocket. Genuine ones include the propulsion unit of the German V2 used against the British in World War

II. Several scientific satellites can be seen, and the multi-layered space suit worn by William A Anders, one of the first men to make a flight round the moon on the Apollo 8 mission, 1968.

This floor also houses the collections related to physics.

In the museum's basement is the Children's Gallery, particularly rich in working models and dioramas. These deal with the sun and the earth, lighting, the measurement of time, heat, pulleys, vacuums, transport and communications. There are exhibitions of fire-making appliances and of the development of locks and fastenings, also a display showing the effects of the introduction of science and technology in the home over many years. Both young and old will find the replica of a kitchen and bathroom of the 1880s fascinating.

Public lectures are given in the Science Museum on most Tuesday, Thursday and Saturday afternoons, and there is a programme of films of general scientific interest. Special lectures for schools and members of the public are also given, bookable in advance. A free leaflet is available from the museum which gives details of the film and lecture programmes. Also available is a free leaflet, *Party Visits,* for the guidance of teachers and other party organisers.

Practical details: Open Monday to Saturday from 10 am to 6 pm and on Sunday from 2.30 to 6 pm. Free admission. Nearest Underground station is South Kensington. Use buses 14, 30, 52, 73 or 74. Refreshments available.

Address: Exhibition Road, South Kensington SW7 2DD. Telephone (01) 589 3456.

SIR JOHN SOANE'S MUSEUM

A haven for architects

Sir John was a passionate collector of *objets,* strange and interesting. His house is full of surprises

Sir John Soane, a noted architect of the Georgian period, designed many buildings all over the country. Some of his houses are still standing, but his most important London building — the Bank of England — has been demolished except for the outer walls. Soane was born in 1753, the son of a builder, and spent two years studying in Italy. In 1812 he built the house in Lincoln's Inn Fields, where he installed his large and fascinatingly diverse collection, formed over the previous 20 years.

At first glance, there seems hardly space for anything more among the orderly clutter of busts, vases, urns and plaster casts which greet one at every turn in the passages. But it is easy to find one's way through, surprise following surprise, whether it is a Canaletto, a Reynolds, a Watteau or a Turner drawing, or a group of beautiful Roman fragments.

Being an architect, Sir John was aware of the value of optical illusion. In the Library, the mirrors above the bookcases give the impression of an extra room on either side.

He cleverly contrived the Picture Room so as to display pictures which would normally fill a gallery three times its size. He layered the walls with folding screens on which paintings were hung — in this case two highly valuable series by William Hogarth, *The Election* and *The Rake's Progress*, of four and eight pictures respectively. It is worth a few minutes' scrutiny to follow through the stories they tell, for Hogarth was a master of detail, everyone in a picture being given an individual character, an activity or an attitude.

Behind two of these screens are Soane's drawings and a model of the Bank of England, with an intriguing view down into a curious room called the Monks' Parlour, and beyond to the Monks' Yard, where stands a stone monument to Soane's favourite dog. 'Alas, Poor Fanny', says the inscription. The two Gothic arches behind this are from the old House of Lords, and legend has it that it was through these arches that Guy Fawkes passed to store his faggots and explosives in the 1605 Gunpowder Plot.

One of the Museum's great treasures is in the Sepulchral Chamber — the alabaster sarcophagus of Seti I. It was discovered in the Valley of the Kings in 1813 by G B Belzoni, whose patron offered it in vain to the British Museum for £2,000. It was bought by Sir John for the same price. It is a wonderful piece of work with carefully inscribed hieroglyphics, at one time inlaid with blue, covering the interior and exterior.

Practical details: Open Tuesday to Saturday from 10 am to 5 pm. There is a public lecture tour every Saturday at 2.30 pm. Free admission. Nearest Underground station is Holborn. Use buses 8, 22, 25 or 68.

Address: 13 Lincoln's Inn Fields WC2A 3BP. Telephone (01) 405 2107.

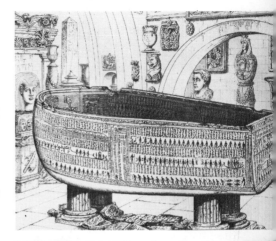

Top: One of the great treasures of the museum, the sarcophagus of Seti I, discovered in the Valley of the Kings in 1813.
Above: A profusion of busts, vases, urns and plaster casts.

SYON HOUSE

Almost a piece of Ancient Rome

Summer home of the Duke and Duchess of Northumberland, and once of Catherine Howard and Lady Jane Grey

Syon House has frequently figured in history. Henry V established a monastery there in 1415, only for it to be suppressed by Henry VIII in 1539; Catherine Howard, his queen, was confined at Syon before being executed. Here, too, Lady Jane Grey was offered the Crown, which she reluctantly accepted.

In the sixteenth century the house passed into the Percy family, who had the pleasure grounds — notable for its rare trees and shrubs — and the park laid out by Capability Brown, and his design has been largely preserved. About 55 acres of Syon Park are now a national centre for gardening.

The interior of the house — 'Ancient Rome in Middlesex' John Betjeman has called it — was transformed by Robert Adam. His work is seen at its glorious best in the Great Hall, with its exquisite ceiling mouldings by Joseph Rose, a screen of Doric columns, four antique marble statues on pedestals from Rome, and a bronze copy of the *Dying Gaul*.

The Roman style is continued in the adjacent Ante Room with its rich colouring and gilding. It has a dozen columns and pilasters — some of them scagliola reproductions, and others of verde-antique brought to Syon after being raised from the bed of the Tiber. The dining-room and red drawing-room, so-called because its walls are hung with crimson Spitalfields silk, are also by Adam. The drawing-room has medallions by Cipriani (who painted the panels in the Gold State Coach) set in gilded bands in the ceiling, some exquisite applied ormolu work by Matthew Boulton, the master craftsman who later became James Watt's partner, two Adam side tables topped with Roman mosaic, and Stuart portraits including works by Van Dyck and Lely.

The Long Gallery is certainly well named — 136 feet long and only 14 feet high and wide. Adam strove to reduce the effect of length by using a series of four pilasters (painted by Michaelangelo Pergolesi) and crossed lines on the ceiling to give the illusion of width. Much of the furniture was designed by Adam specially for this room.

Practical details: The house is open daily over Easter. From Easter to September it is open from Sunday to Thursday, 12 noon to 5 pm, and the rest of the year on Sunday only, from 12 noon to 5 pm. There is an admission charge, but organised parties who book in advance will get a reduction. The gardens are open daily all year round, except over Christmas, from 10 am to 6 pm. During winter they close at dusk. There is an admission charge (but the Garden Centre is free). Nearby British Rail stations are Kew Bridge (SR) and Twickenham (SR). Nearby Underground stations are Gunnersbury and Hammersmith. Use buses 37, 65, 117, 237, 267, E1 or E2.
Address: Brentford, Middlesex TW8 8JF. Telephone (01) 560 0884.

THE TATE GALLERY

10,000 works of art

The riverside gallery, founded by a sugar millionaire, houses two of the most important national collections

The Tate Gallery was opened in 1897 on its Thames-side site in response to a need for a fuller representation of the British school of art than could be offered by the National Gallery (page 107). It is named after Henry (later Sir Henry) Tate, the sugar millionaire, who was its founder and principal benefactor.

It contains two national collections: British paintings from the sixteenth century to the turn of the century, and British and foreign modern paintings and sculpture.

The galleries, in chronological order, begin with British paintings of the sixteenth and seventeenth centuries. There is a strong representation of the works of William Hogarth (1697-1764), including his first major success, *A Scene from the Beggars' Opera,* and his famous self-portrait with his pug.

Several galleries are given over to the works of J M W Turner, the greatest of British painters. Turner left around 300 oils and 19,000 watercolours and drawings to the national collection (almost all the watercolours are housed at the British Museum). This vast stock is liberally drawn upon, making it possible to trace Turner's development from his early sketches

'The Family Group', by Henry Moore. The Gallery houses one of the foremost art collections in the country.

from nature to his late works, where his subjects seem almost subordinate to his brilliant handling of light and colour.

A showcase in the Turner galleries contains items from his studio, including his palettes, paints, model boats — ships and the sea fascinated him — jars of pigment, and his paintbox.

John Constable, father of English landscape painting, who was appreciated more in France than in England in his lifetime, is also well represented. These include *View at Epsom, Flatford Mill* and a number of full-scale sketches for more complete versions, such as *Dedham Mill.*

The Tate also has the most representative collection in the world of works by the visionary poet and painter William Blake, including many of the illustrations to Dante's *Divine Comedy* and his rare tempera paintings.

The Tate's collection of modern foreign art begins with the Impressionists and Post-Impressionists, taking in Pissarro, Sisley, Monet, Van Gogh, Degas, Cézanne, Renoir and Gauguin. It continues through Braque, Picasso, Futurism, Surrealism to postwar European and American art, including Abstract Expressionism and Pop. Masterpieces on display include Picasso's *The Three Dancers* and Matisse's *L'Escargot* (The Snail). British art since 1880 includes pictures by Beardsley, Sickert, Augustus John, Sir Stanley Spencer, Paul Nash, Henry Moore, Graham Sutherland, John Piper and Francis Bacon.

Sculptures include Rodin's *The Kiss* (1886), often considered his masterpiece, and works by Epstein, Henry Moore, Barbara Hepworth, Giacometti and Maillol.

The Tate possesses about 6,000 paintings and sculptures and about 4,000 prints. Only a proportion of these works can be displayed at any one time because of limited accommodation. 50 per cent more exhibition space is being provided by the major extension due to open in May 1979.

A regular programme of free lectures, guided tours and films is arranged.

Practical details: Open Monday to Saturday from 10 am to 6 pm and on Sunday from 2 to 6 pm. Free admission. Nearest British Rail station is Victoria (SR) and nearest Underground station is Pimlico. Use buses 2, 2B, 3, 36, 36B, 77, 88, 185 or 507. Refreshments available.

Address: Millbank SW1P 4RG. Telephone (01) 821 1313. For recorded information telephone (01) 821 7128.

THE THOMAS CORAM FOUNDATION FOR CHILDREN

The story of a captain's compassion

Paintings by Hogarth, one of the early governors, are among the Foundation's many treasures

When Thomas Coram, sea captain and shipbuilder, returned from America, he was shocked by the number of children, usually illegitimate, who were left by their parents to die. Out of compassion for such children, the Foundling Hospital was established in 1739 to care for and educate them.

Today, the hospital is no more, but Coram's work continues. There is an adoption and foster-care service for the placement of children with special needs, and a Children's Centre. Among the first governors of the original hospital was William Hogarth, father of modern English painting, who with his wife became a foster parent himself (Hogarth designed the Foundation's coat of arms, which is still in use). Three fine pictures by Hogarth are among the Foundation's treasures, including one of Thomas Coram himself — the first truly realistic portrait of a commoner, as distinct from the often romanticized work of the court painters.

Another Hogarth, *The March of the Guards to Finchley, 1746* is set in Tottenham Court Road. The third picture is an engraving of *Moses*

Brought Before Pharaoh's Daughter dated 1751.

Other works are by Richard and Benjamin Wilson, Francis Hayman, Thomas Gainsborough, Sir John Millais, Sir Joshua Reynolds and Allan Ramsay, most of whom became Governors. There is also a cartoon by Raphael, *The Massacre of the Innocents*, the largest remaining fragment of one of twelve cartoons for a series of tapestries depicting scenes from Christ's life.

Among the Foundation's early benefactors was the great composer George Frederick Handel, who though German-born became a British subject in 1726. He presented the hospital with its first chapel organ, on which he gave the first performance of his masterpiece, *Messiah,* in England in 1750. Among the relics on show is the organ keyboard, a terracotta bust of Handel by Roubiliac, and one of three fair copies made of the *Messiah* score.

The Foundation's art collection has an interesting link with another British institution. In 1759, at the annual artists' feast held in the hospital, Hayman proposed the founding of 'a great museum all our own'. This led to the holding of an annual exhibition and the founding of the Royal Academy.

Practical details: Open Monday to Friday from 10 am to 4 pm (except when conferences are taking place). There is an admission charge. Nearby British Rail stations are King's Cross (ER) and St Pancras (ER). Nearby Underground stations are King's Cross and Russell Square. Use buses 14, 30, 68 or 73.

Address: 40 Brunswick Square WC1N 1AZ. Telephone (01) 278 2424.

THE TOWER OF LONDON

The Crown Jewels

England's oldest museum — the Armouries, with Henry VIII's armour; the glittering beauty of the Crown Jewels; and a regimental museum containing nine VCs

The White Tower, the oldest part of the Tower of London, was built by William the Conqueror, not as a defence against foreign invaders but as a protection against unruly Londoners. Today Londoners, as well as foreign and provincial visitors, can pay a peaceful visit to the White Tower, which houses the Armouries. This, the national museum of arms and armour dating from before 1660, can count itself the oldest museum in England.

On the first floor is the Sporting Gallery, which displays sporting weapons, including firearms, used between the Middle Ages and the end of the 1800s. Among them is a variety of crossbows, many of them beautifully decorated, and a case of multi-shot guns, some with as many as seven barrels. Not to be missed is the fine hunting suite of arms belonging to Duke Ernst August of Saxe-Weimar (1688-1749), with rifle, pistols and powder flask.

The age of chivalry is recalled by exhibits in the Tournament Gallery, where jousting armour used in the fifteenth and sixteenth centuries is on show. A much-prized piece is the late-fifteenth-century armour for the *Scharfrennen,* a kind of joust using sharp lances.

Exhibits ranging from the knives and axes of the Vikings to the armour of the fifteenth century are shown in the Medieval Gallery, where one of the finest pieces is the armour for man and horse, made in South Germany in 1480. In the Sixteenth Century Gallery are two bow-staves, almost the only surviving examples of this historic weapon, raised last century from the *Mary Rose,* one of Henry VIII's ships. Also worth looking out for is the field armour, dating from about 1535-40. Made for a giant of a man, a German, 6 feet 10 inches tall, it is an unforgettable sight.

The Royal Armour Gallery was once the White Tower's Council Chamber. Here is the magnificent collection of Henry VIII's armour.

More Royal armour can be seen in the Seventeenth Century Gallery, including the gilt harness (another name for armour) of Charles I, traditionally the gift of the City of London, and Charles II's highly decorated suit used when he was Prince of Wales.

Down in the basement are the Mortar and Cannon Rooms, which once housed the rack for torturing prisoners but now contains many pieces of historic ordnance: muskets, rifles, swords, lances, helmets and cuirasses. There are also sixteenth- and seventeenth-century cannon, including guns raised from the ocean

Elephant armour, probably a trophy of the Battle of Plassey, 1757, brought home by Lord Clive.

bed (there is one from the *Mary Rose),* and some bronze guns made for Henry VIII. On the walls are many hand weapons of the period, including long pikes, halberds and bills.

The new Armouries, a short distance from the White Tower, contain a collection of Oriental arms and armour, which offers an interesting comparison in style with the European armour in the White Tower. The centrepiece among the armour here is a suit for an elephant, composed of hundreds of small overlapping steel plates. It is probably of Hindu origin and was brought back from India by Lord Clive.

THE CROWN JEWELS

The Jewel House, situated at the west end of the Waterloo Barracks block, is the Tower's greatest attraction; for here are displayed, in all their glittering glory, the Crown Jewels. After Charles I's execution, royal ornaments were melted down by

144

Cromwell, and therefore the treasures here date mostly from the reign of Charles II. On the ground floor are cases containing maces, dishes, salt cellars, an alms dish, ewer and basin, chalices and a wine cooler — all of silver-gilt; and a set of 10 silver state trumpets, dating from 1780, most of them still with their banners bearing the Royal Arms.

Also displayed are gowns and insignia of the great Orders of Knighthood: Garter, Bath, St Michael & St George, Victorian Order, Thistle, and British Empire; also the highest awards for gallantry, the Victoria Cross and George Cross.

Nearby are the Sovereign's gold-embroidered Coronation robes.

The Crown of England, made for King Charles II and used for the actual ceremony of crowning.

Downstairs in the basement are the Crown Jewels, displayed in a central case lit to show them in their full splendour. The most important single item is St Edward's Crown, with which the Sovereign is crowned at the Coronation. It weighs five pounds and is of gold, set with rubies, emeralds and diamonds.

More ornate is the heavily jewel-encrusted Imperial State Crown, which the monarch wears while returning from Westminster Abbey after the Coronation. It is also worn on state occasions, such as the Opening of Parliament. Among its array of jewels is the Black Prince's Ruby, a gift to the Prince, it is believed, in 1367, and worn by Henry V in his helmet-crown at the Battle of Agincourt.

All the Coronation regalia is on show, including the ampulla and spoon used in the anointing ceremony (they are the oldest objects here), the Sword and Spurs, Orb and Sceptre with the Cross, and Sceptre with the Dove. The former sceptre signifies kingly rule and contains a huge 530-carat diamond — the largest cut diamond in the world.

Several other crowns are on show, including Queen Victoria's small crown, the one made for the Prince of Wales in 1729, and the crowns of Queen Elizabeth the Queen Mother (which contains the Koh-i-noor diamond), the late Queen Mary, and the one worn by King George V at the great Delhi Durbar in 1911.

ROYAL FUSILIERS MUSEUM

This museum covers the period from 1685, when the Royal Fusiliers (City of London Regiment) were raised on the authority of James II by the then Constable of the Tower of London, until 1968. Then the Royal Fusiliers joined the three other English Fusilier Regiments to form the Royal Regiment of Fusiliers.

In Room I of the museum is the flint-lock musket, or 'fusil', with which the regiment was first armed. Its original task was to defend the guns of the artillery against attack.·

In this room and Rooms II and III are dioramas of Albuhera (1811), Alma (1854), Mons (1914), in which the first two Victoria Crosses of the war were won by the regiment, and Casino (1944) — battles in which the Fusiliers played a distinctive part.

In Room II, covering 1854-1918, are nine Victoria Crosses and the original one struck in 1856 for the Queen's inspection and approval; the uniform of King George V as Colonel-in-Chief of the regiment 1900-36, and battle relics of the Crimean and Boer Wars. The story is brought up to date in Room III with exhibits including officers' commissions signed by every monarch since George IV, a set of horse furniture given to the Duke of Kent, Colonel-in-Chief until his death in an air crash in 1942, and reminders of the regiment's service in Korea.

Practical details: The Armouries, Jewel House and Fusiliers Museum are open between March and October, Monday to Saturday from 9.30 am to 5 pm and on Sunday from 2 to 5 pm. Between November and February they are open Monday to Saturday from 9.30 am to 4 pm and closed on Sunday. There is an admission charge to each. Nearest British Rail station is Fenchurch Street (ER) and nearest Underground station is Tower Hill. Use buses 9, 9A, 10, 40, 42, 44 or 78. **Address:** Tower Hill EC3N 4AB. Telephone: (01) 709 0765.

VERULAMIUM MUSEUM

A Roman city uncovered

A host of archaeological finds that tell us of art and life 1,500 years ago

Visitors to this museum will be within a stone's throw of the basilica, the public centre of the old Roman city of Verulamium (now St Albans) which existed for five centuries. Much of it, but by no means all, has been excavated.

In the museum are most of the results of this work, and some of the items are remarkably beautiful. For example, the large and famous mosaics displayed on the wall opposite the museum entrance, the geometric pavement, the Sea God — or Neptune — mosaic, and the Shell — a tessellated pavement with the design of a scallop shell.

A number of Romano-British coffins containing skeletons have been found, and four of these, containing a man, woman and two children, can be seen. The museum's central feature is a relief model of the Roman city as it was, complete with houses, temples, shops, municipal buildings such as the basilica, and a triumphal arch. There is an enlarged model of the south-east, or London, gate, nearby. Verulamium was a civil settlement, but local discoveries have included a first-century legionary's helmet in excellent condition, and many other small military accoutrements.

Many panels suggest the kind of

everyday lives that the Romans led, with displays of cooking utensils, jugs, flagons; their building methods, with windows, wall and floor decorations. Visitors can see many household items, including locks and keys with diagrams showing how they worked, and an interesting collection of Roman coins.

The gallery next to the main museum offers reconstructions of Roman kitchen methods and shows the kind of food they ate: oysters, dates, bread, grapes. There are displays of jewellery and toilet accessories, such as as ear-picks and nail cleaners, and fragments of a shoe.

Articles bearing the figures of gods and goddesses worshipped by Roman religious cults can be seen, along with instruments associated with trades and professions: needles, balances, spatulas, forceps, pruning hooks, a carpenter's plane.

Some parts of the Roman city can still be seen *in situ*, including a small portion of the basilica, the hypocaust (housed in the centre of the park), the south-east gate of the city, a well-preserved run of town wall, and the theatre (about 100 yards away from the museum, and administered separately).

Practical details: Open Monday to Saturday from 10 am to 5.30 pm and on Sunday from 2 to 5.30 pm. Between October and March the closing time is 4 pm. There is an admission charge. Nearest British Rail station is St Albans (ER). Use buses 84 or 330, or Green Line coaches 707, 717, 724 or 727. Easy parking. Open spaces nearby.

Address: St Michael's Street, St Albans, Hertfordshire AS3 4SW. Telephone St Albans 54649.

VICTORIA AND ALBERT MUSEUM

The nation's finest treasures

You could spend a week in the V & A and never see it all

The 'V & A', whose originator was Prince Albert, Queen Victoria's consort, possesses the noblest and most extensive collection of fine and applied art in Britain. The foundation stone of the present building was laid in 1899 by Queen Victoria and it was opened by King Edward VII ten years later.

So rich and vast is this museum that it is an impossible task to see it in its entirety all at once. There are only two satisfactory ways to see the 'V & A'. One is to tour the primary galleries, where the museum's exhibits are collected together by period, style and nationality. The second is to spend one's time seeing a few selected departmental study collections, comprising architecture and sculpture, ceramics, furniture and woodwork, metalwork, Oriental, Far Eastern, paintings and drawings, and textiles.

A good starting point is Room 43, which is devoted to medieval art and is straight ahead from the main entrance. In one of the central cases is the Eltenburg reliquary, a splendidly beautiful example of Romanesque coppersmith's craftsmanship, shaped like a domed church and made in Cologne about AD 1180. It was saved by a Dutch nun from her nunnery during the Revolutionary Wars. To the right is the ninth century Easby Cross, made of sandstone from Easby Abbey in Yorkshire.

Rooms 23-9, containing Gothic art and tapestry, offer fine examples of English medieval embroidery — the Clare Chasuble, in silver-gilt and silver thread, and two great copes (Room 23). In Room 25, one of the most imposing items is a large Valencian altar-piece dated about AD 1410. In tempera and gilt on pinewood, it shows often grisly scenes from the story of St George.

The four huge tapestries in Room 38, boldly coloured and interesting for their lack of perspective, show medieval hunting scenes; they are thought to have been brought to England from Tournai at the time of Henry VI's marriage.

The 'V & A' has a wonderful collection of Italian Renaissance art, and there are some fine sculptures in Room 16. Farther on in Room 14 there is a large armorial by Luca della Robbia in polychrome enamelled terracotta. A dozen others by the same artist, in Room 12, depict the Labours of the Months. Not to be missed either here is a collection of terracotta sketch models.

In the Renaissance rooms, two groups of sculpture should not be passed by: *Samson and Philistine* by Giovanni Bologna, and, at the top of some steps near the Costume Court, Bernini's *Neptune and Triton*.

The Costume Court houses one of the finest collections of dress in the world: 120 items representing the mainstream of fashion between 1580 and 1947, both English and Continental. There are also 600 accessories, such as hats and gloves, fans, shoes, bustles and underwear. Costume Court is circular and the historical sequence begins in the north-east corner, with the older exhibits in the centre and the later ones round the circumference. The earliest man's costume on show is a doublet and hose said to have been worn by James I on the day before his Coronation, and there is another embroidered doublet which belonged to Charles I.

Sir Cecil Beaton presented the museum with a great collection of costumes of the present century, and these are exhibited from time to time. Other costumes are in store.

Upstairs from Costume Court is the Musical Instruments Gallery, which includes the earliest known

harpsichord of certain date (1521), four Italian spinets of this period, and a beautifully carved violin said to have belonged to Charles II. One of the curious instruments here is the 'giraffe piano', equipped with drum and bells and resembling a grand piano on end, dated around 1810. Recordings of the instruments can be heard in the gallery.

Outside the entrance to Costume Court is the museum's strangest work of 'art' and certainly the most gruesome: *Tippoo's Tiger*.

Nearby, in Room 48, are the Raphael cartoons, which fill the walls of one large gallery. Raphael painted them in 1515 as designs for tapestries for the Sistine Chapel, in Rome. Charles I of England, when Prince of Wales,

bought them in 1623, and Queen Victoria lent them to the 'V & A' in 1865. They have been on loan ever since. First of a series of four, all with a biblical theme, is the *Miraculous Draught of Fishes*. This was

---

One of the Victoria and Albert's strangest exhibits — and certainly the most gruesome: Tippoo's Tiger. This was the plaything of Tippoo Sultan in India and obviously the product of a warped sense of humour. It is a mechanical organ, made about 1790 and encased in a wooden tiger with its teeth sunk in the neck of an East India Company officer. The miniature organ keyboard and bellows inside the Tiger reproduce the cries of the dying victim.

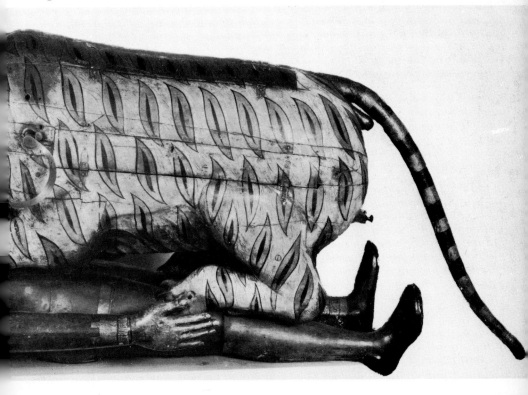

Bernini's 'Neptune and Triton', in the Renaissance rooms at the Victoria and Albert.

completed as a tapestry, being made in Mortlake tapestry works after Prince Charles had bought the cartoons. Three cartoons opposite show scenes from St Paul's life.

The British Art section begins in Room 52 with the Tudor period. A spinet belonging to Queen Elizabeth, and bearing her badge, is on show, and the famous Great Bed of Ware of about 1580, which could accommodate four couples.

Two items which belonged to Charles I are in Room 53: a military scarf worn at Edgehill, and the chair he is assumed to have used at his trial. Tapestries, furniture, embroidery and miniatures are also to be seen here. Among the exhibits is a part of the Oxburgh Hangings, made by Mary, Queen of Scots and Bess of Hardwick in 1570.

Upstairs, Room 126 and the eight rooms following cover British art in 1750-1900: English japanned furniture, woven and brocaded silk from Spitalfields, pottery, porcelain from Chelsea, Bow, Derby and Longton Hall. One outstanding item is part of the glass drawing-room from Northumberland House, London, which was designed by Robert Adam. Room 119 shows a selection of William Morris's work (see William Morris Gallery, page 158).

The museum's paintings are to the right of the main entrance; in Rooms 8 and 9. Here is assembled a remarkable collection of nearly 400 pictures by the landscape painter, John Constable, presented to the museum by his daughter Isabel in 1888.

There is a full and varied programme of lectures. Details are available from the Education Department, which also arranges conducted lectures.

Practical details: Open Monday to Thursday, and Saturday, from 10 am to 5.50 pm. Also on Sunday from 2.30 to 5.50 pm. Free admission. Nearest Underground station is South Kensington. Use buses 14, 30, 49 or 74. Refreshments available.

Address: South Kensington SW7 2RL. Telephone (01) 589 6371.

THE WALLACE COLLECTION

Family treasures

Arms and armour, pictures and porcelain, craftsmanship of all kinds — a gift to the nation

The Wallace Collection is one of the richest and most varied repositories of pictures and art objects that has ever been privately accumulated in Britain. It was bequeathed to the nation by Lady Wallace, who died in 1897. Her husband, Sir Richard Wallace, had extended the collection left to him by his father, the fourth Marquess of Hertford. It is now housed in Hertford House, which was for many years the Wallaces' home.

There is plenty to catch the eye: furniture, often ornate and beautifully inlaid, pictures, clocks, porcelain, bronze statuettes, arms and armour . . . Many of these are to be seen in Galleries I and II, where there are also two rare and impressive chandeliers made by Jacques Caffièri, perhaps for a member of the French royal family.

In the next gallery there is some early French furniture, and the boxwood Hercules carved by Francesco da Sant'Agata in 1520, as well as a large collection of Italian majolica in the wall cases. The most imposing item is the Bath of Maidens dish of 1525.

An interesting item in Gallery IV is the Bell of Mura, dating from the seventh century, made of bronze with Celtic tracery and decorated with semi-precious stones. The bell is of Irish origin, and was at one time credited with healing properties. The Horn of St Hubert, below it, is

The Wallace Collection contains the original of 'The Laughing Cavalier', by Hals.

thought to have been a present from the Bishop of Liege to the Duke of Burgundy as a token of appreciation for suppressing a local rising in 1468. A fine collection of European arms and armour can be seen in Galleries V, VI and VII. In the first of these the central feature is the equestrian armour made for the Count Palatine of the Rhine early in the 1500s. In the second, the Italian bronze cannon, beautifully decorated with mythological scenes in high relief, catches the eye. The centrepiece, however, is the fifteenth-century war harness (armour) for horse and man: a

Detail from 'The Swing', by Fragonard.

first-class example of German Gothic craftsmanship.

In the corridor between Galleries IX and X are some excellent water-colours by Richard Parkes Bonington, and four early ones by J M W Turner — an interesting contrast with his later work.

In Gallery X is an impressive wardrobe by Boulle. Its oak body is veneered with ebony, with marquetry in brass and tortoise-shell, and with reliefs of gilt-bronze.

Gallery XI is notable for its Murillo paintings, in particular the *Adoration of the Shepherds, Joseph and his Brethren* and the *Marriage of the Virgin*. There is also a Holbein self-portrait among the fine collection of largely eighteenth-century miniatures.

The first-floor galleries are reached by the marble staircase, with its iron and bronze, chased and gilt balustrade.

The walls bear noteworthy works by Francois Boucher, two canvases of *The Rising and Setting of the Sun,* owned at one time by Madame de Pompadour.

More first-class paintings, by Guardi, including four views of Venice, are to be seen in Gallery XII, and two cases of Sèvres porcelain, including a magnificent boat-shaped pot-pourri vase. The eighteenth-century *regulateur* clock, with its gilt-bronze mounts, shows Greenwich mean time, true solar time, phases, age and longitude of the moon; rising, setting of the sun and the date.

Gallery XIII is the first of a series containing notable, often famous, paintings: Rubens' *The Defeat and Death of Maxentius,* for example, and his sketch for *The Adoration of the Magi.*

Gallery XVI is the largest in the house and contains numerous masterpieces. Among them are the huge *Annunciation* by Champaigne, Salvator Rosa's fine *Landscape with*

Apollo and the Cumaean Sibyl, the world-famous *Laughing Cavalier* by Frans Hals, of 1624, and Van Dyck's *Philippe Le Roy, Seigneur de Ravels.* Thomas Gainsborough's beautiful portrait, *Mrs Robinson,* known as *Perdita,* shows his subject seated in a landscape.

Other memorable pictures in this gallery are Rubens' magnificent *Rainbow Landscape,* painted near Brussels; Rembrandt's *Titus;* Velazquez's *A Lady with a Fan;* and Watteau's *The Halt during the Chase.* Two more Watteau masterpieces, *Music Party* and *A Lady at her Toilet,* are in Gallery XVIII, along with Fragonard's well-known picture, *The Swing.* Among the exhibits also in Gallery XVIII, and in XIX, is a collection of about 90 gold boxes, demonstrating many different styles of exquisite craftsmanship.

In the next gallery hangs Boucher's celebrated portrait, *Madame de Pompadour.* There are also a beautiful lacquer chest of drawers by Dubois, and an eighteenth-century perfume burner in red jasper made by Pierre Gouthiere, which was at one time in Marie Antoinette's collection. The adjacent corridor features a magnificent German 55-piece travelling canteen of silver-gilt of the eighteenth century.

Practical details: Open Monday to Saturday from 10 am to 5 pm and on Sunday from 2 to 5 pm. Free admission. Nearby Underground stations are Bond Street and Baker Street. Use buses 2, 2B, 6, 8, 12, 15, 30, 73, 74, 88 or 137.

Address: Hertford House, Manchester Square W1M 6BN. Telephone (01) 935 0687.

WELLINGTON MUSEUM

Conquering hero

Mementoes of one of Britain's greatest military leaders . . . his honours, treasures, and scribbled orders on the field of Waterloo

Known as 'No 1 London', possibly because it would have been the first house encountered when travelling eastwards into the capital, Apsley House was for 35 years the home of the first Duke of Wellington, hero of Waterloo and for a time Prime Minister. Apsley House was designed by Robert Adam and altered in 1828-30 by Benjamin Wyatt. It now belongs to the nation, though the present Duke has accommodation there, and it is administered by the Victoria and Albert Museum.

The house contains many fine paintings, including works by Brueghel, Van Dyck, Goya, Van Huysum, Landseer, Sir Joshua Reynolds, Rubens, Velazquez and Vermeer.

The Plate and China Room, the first visitors enter, has three large pieces of silver-gilt plate — a gift to the first Duke from the City of London's merchants and bankers. One of them is the Wellington Shield, which shows the Duke mounted on a horse, with the allegorical figure of Victory. The sections show scenes from the Duke's campaigns.

A case on the wall displays 16 swords and daggers, including a French sabre that was carried by Wellington at Waterloo. This famous battle was fought near Brussels in 1815, when the Duke, with Prussian support, defeated

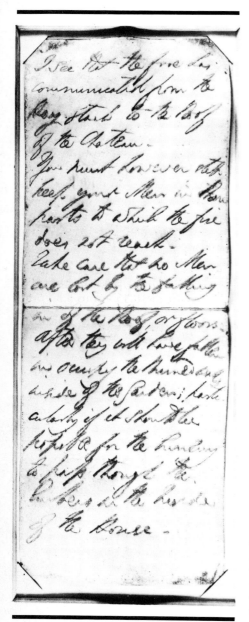

A handwritten despatch by the Duke of Wellington, from the Battle of Waterloo.

the French who were led by Napoleon. Of the ten batons nearby, three signify the rank of field-marshal of the British Army, one of them being in gold and presented to the Duke by the Prince Regent.

Among the Duke's personal possessions on display are the pieces of ass's skin on which could be pencilled orders to his unit commanders, then erased. The orders on show were written at Waterloo.

In the basement is a reference collection of engravings and caricatures, including scenes of the Duke's funeral. The staircase vestibule is the setting for an imposing nude statue of Napoleon Buonaparte. More than 11 feet high, it was sculpted from a single block of marble by an Italian, Antonio Canova. Napoleon disliked this work because the figure of Victory in the statue's right hand appears to be turning away from him. George IV presented it to Wellington the year after Waterloo.

The Mattei bust of Cicero, a Greek work of the first century BC, is on the first-floor landing at the top of the main staircase, with several pictures including two of Pensioners at Greenwich and Chelsea, the latter reading the Waterloo despatch with obvious pleasure.

The Piccadilly Drawing-Room, which overlooks Piccadilly itself, contains Adam decor and the original fireplace. The cut-glass chandelier was here in the Duke's day.

Correggio's *The Agony in the Garden* was the Duke's favourite painting, which he had captured from Joseph Buonaparte's baggage train at Vitoria, Spain, two years before Waterloo.

In the magnificent Waterloo Gallery, reached through the Portico Room, the Duke held his Waterloo Banquets between 1830 and his death in 1852. But at least ten earlier Banquets were held in the Dining Room, where the beautiful silver and silver-gilt centrepiece of the Portuguese Service, 26 feet long, used at the banquets, can be seen. It was originally made up of a thousand pieces and was given to Wellington by the Regent of Portugal. The ornament at the centre symbolises the continents of Europe, America, Asia and Africa.

In the Striped Drawing-Room there is an excellent painting of the Battle of Waterloo by Sir William Allan, RA. The Duke approved it warmly, with the comment: 'Good — very good; not too much smoke!'

Practical details: Open Tuesday, Wednesday, Thursday and Saturday from 10 am to 6 pm and on Sunday from 2.30 to 6 pm. Free admission. Nearest Underground station is Hyde Park Corner. Use buses 2, 2B, 14, 16, 16A, 19, 22, 30, 36B, 38, 52, 73, 74 or 137.

Address: Apsley House, 149 Piccadilly W1V 9FA. Telephone (01) 499 5676.

THE FUNERAL CARRIAGE (ST PAUL'S CATHEDRAL CRYPT)

The funeral of the Duke of Wellington in 1852 was the biggest in history, and the procession was watched by one and a half million people who lined the route from the Royal Hospital, Chelsea (page 126), where he lay in state, to St Paul's Cathedral, where he is buried.

The funeral carriage, which was drawn by 12 black draught horses,

three abreast, now stands in the crypt of St Paul's Cathedral, along with the Duke's tomb, in virtually the same grotesque splendour as the day it was used. The main part is of metal melted down from guns captured at Waterloo. It weighs, in all, 18 tons. On the sides are the Duke's battle honours, with ornamentation, painted in gilt.

A contemporary engraving near the carriage captures the atmosphere of the scene on the day of the funeral. The carriage was made in 18 days by 100 men working in two shifts. In 1973 it was overhauled and repaired by 31 officers and men at the Royal School of Military Engineering at Chatham.

Practical details: Open Monday to Saturday from 10.45 am to 3.30 pm. There is an admission charge. Nearby Underground stations are St Paul's and Blackfriars. Use buses 6, 9, 11, 15, 17, 18, 45, 46 or 63.

Address: Near Ludgate Hill, London EC4.

The grotesque splendour of the Duke of Wellington's 18-ton Funeral Carriage, in St. Paul's Cathedral crypt.

WESLEY'S HOUSE

The world... my parish

The home of John Wesley, evangelist and founder of Methodism, and his personal possessions

John Wesley's house stands quietly next to his chapel, which has been described as the 'cathedral of World Methodism'.

It remains much as it was, with many of Wesley's personal belongings and furniture still to be seen. In his study is his 'straddle' chair with its book rest (which is supposed to have been given him by a cockfighting bookmaker whom he had converted to Christianity); his bureau, in walnut with secret drawers; umbrella; grandfather clock; preaching gown; cravat and three-cornered hat.

Wesley died in the bedroom, with the words 'The best of all is, God is with us' all but the last on his lips. Adjoining the bedroom is his prayer room, with chair and little walnut table.

In the museum room is a case full of personal possessions: his spurs (he rode around the country preaching), spectacles, and the pen with which he wrote his last letter — to William Wilberforce, the slave-trade reformer, commending his efforts. Also displayed are the gown, coat and hat in which he was baptized in 1703, his nightcap and Bible.

The room contains Wesley's lectern, which he used in the Foundery building before the present chapel was built, and a huge one-gallon teapot, the gift of Josiah Wedgwood. It bears the verse:

Be present at our table, Lord
Be here and everywhere ador'd
These creatures bless & grant that we
May feast in Paradise with thee.

Alongside this is a glass bust of Wesley dated about 1780 (these are very rare: there are only two other examples of glass busts in existence).

One of the 417 books that Wesley either wrote or published was *Primitive Physic*. He was deeply interested in medicine, and he designed an electrical machine for 'treating' at least 35 illnesses, including melancholia, falling sickness, rheumatism, shingles and toothache among his patients in the Foundery, where he established the first free medical clinic in England. The electrical machine is on show in the house.

John Wesley's brother Charles is commemorated in his own bedroom. Charles is best known as the prolific writer of more than 5,000 hymns.

Wesley's tomb is behind the house and chapel. Opposite the chapel is the famous burial ground of Bunhill Fields, where are buried Wesley's mother Susannah, and a number of famous people in art and literature, among them Daniel Defoe, William Blake, John Bunyan and Isaac Watts.

Practical details: Open Monday to Saturday from 10 am to 1 pm and from 2 to 4 pm. There is an admission charge. Nearby Underground stations are Moorgate and Old Street. Use buses 5, 43, 55, 76, 104, 141, 214 or 271.

Address: 47 City Road EC1Y 1AV. Telephone (01) 253 2262.

156

WESTMINSTER ABBEY TREASURES

Funeral effigies of kings and queens

Likenesses in wood, plaster and wax, of people from the past

In the Norman Undercroft of Westminster Abbey, the oldest remaining part above ground of the original abbey buildings of Edward the Confessor, is a permanent exhibition of funeral effigies of kings and queens of England and other prominent historical figures. The entrance to the exhibition is from the Dark Cloister, which leads off the eastern walk of the Great Cloister.

The funeral effigies, made of either wood, plaster or wax, were until the eighteenth century traditionally carried on coffins as they were borne through the streets in funeral processions. The oldest is of Edward III, father of the Black Prince.

Then there are Anne of Bohemia (Richard II's first wife), Katherine de Valois (Henry V's French queen), Elizabeth of York and her husband Henry VII. Last of the 'Ragged Regiment' are Queen Mary I and Anne of Denmark (wife of James I).

Of the later effigies, all costumed, three are especially noteworthy. Of Charles II's effigy, in Garter robes, a chronicler wrote: ' 'Tis to the life, and truly to admiration.' The Duchess of Devonshire felt similarly about Lord

William Pitt, one of the many lifelike effigies in the Norman Undercroft of Westminster Abbey.

Nelson's figure, displayed here, which was 'just as if he was standing there'. But the best of all is probably that of William Pitt, the first Earl of Chatham and Prime Minister, which is unnervingly realistic.

Other wax effigies are of William and

157

Mary, Queen Anne and Frances, Duchess of Richmond. The last two to be carried at funerals were Edmund Sheffield, Duke of Buckingham (died 1735), and his mother, Katherine, Duchess of Buckingham (died 1743), an illegitimate daughter of James II. An effigy of Elizabeth I shows her in a dress modelled on the one she wore to the Thanksgiving Service in the Abbey after the defeat of the Spanish Armada in 1588.

Interspersed with the effigies are items connected with the Abbey's long history: documents, seals, engravings. There are the royal writ and seal of Edward the Confessor, the Abbey's founder, a letter from John of Gaunt, the tournament helm of Henry VII, Henry V's sword, tournament helm and saddle — the earliest surviving complete saddle in Europe.

Two other items worth looking out for are the ring Elizabeth I is said to have given Robert Devereux, Earl of Essex, to be produced if he were at any time in trouble, and an original drawing of the north front, signed by Sir Christopher Wren, when he was the Abbey's architect.

Practical details: Open Monday to Friday from 9.15 am to 5 pm and on Saturday until 5.30 pm. Between April and September it is also open on Sunday, from 9.15 am to 5.30 pm. Tickets are issued up to half-an-hour before closing time. Closed Christmas Day, Boxing Day and Good Friday. There is an admission charge. Nearest British Rail station is Victoria (SR). Nearby Underground stations are St James's Park and Westminster. Use buses 3, 11, 12, 24, 29, 39, 53, 77, 88, 159, 503 or 507.
Address: London SW1P 3PA. Telephone (01) 222 5152.

WILLIAM MORRIS GALLERY

The great craftsman

Examples of the work of William Morris and his movement for the improvement of design

William Morris, poet, socialist, designer and craftsman, was born about half a mile from this house in 1834, at Elm House, Clay Hill, Walthamstow. He founded his own firm for the manufacture of furniture, wallpapers and church decorations. Morris was among the leaders of a movement to make good design available commercially, and he greatly influenced English craftsmanship for the better in his day.

Many examples of his work, and that of his friends, such as Edward Burne-Jones, and his one-time amanuensis, Frank Brangwyn, are on show here. A permanent exhibition describes Morris's life and work, with photographs of where he lived and worked, and places for which his firm provided furnishings, together with cartoons for stained glass, wallpaper and fabrics.

A special section is devoted to the decoration of St James's Palace, for which Morris received a prestigious commission: there are pieces of rose-coloured damask used as a wall covering, and a cartoon and specimen of the richly colourful St James's wallpaper which he designed.

There are also products designed by Morris and members of his firm — tiles, copper candlesticks, and

Among the textiles exhibited are printed cottons and chintzes, and a large tapestry, *The Woodpecker*, woven by the high-warp process which Morris taught himself. Among the gallery's principal exhibits are six large panels, satin stitch on cream silk, exquisitely embroidered by Helen, Lady Lucas-Tooth, shortly after World War I, to Morris's designs.

The artist Frank Brangwyn, who was knighted in 1941, worked in the Morris studio as a textile designer in his youth, and a Royal Doulton dinner service and two cabinets designed by him in the 1930s are on show, together with some of his oil paintings, prints and water-colours.

The gallery also has examples of the work of Morris's contemporaries, such as A H Mackmurdo, founder of the influential Century Guild which worked along the same lines as Morris's company, and the four Martin brothers, who were the first studio potters of the modern English school. They produced their famous and distinctive salt-glazed stoneware (Martinware) until World War I.

Practical details: Open Monday to Saturday from 10 am to 5 pm. Between April and September the closing time is 8 pm on Tuesday and Thursday. It is also open on the first Sunday in each month from 10 am to 12 noon and from 2 to 5 pm. Free admission. Nearest British Rail station is Walthamstow Central (ER) and the nearest Underground station is Blackhorse Road. Use buses 20, 34, 55, 69, 123, 262, 275, 276 or W21, or Green Line coach 702. Open spaces nearby.

Address: Water House, Lloyd Park, Forest Road E17 4PP. Telephone (01) 527 5544 extension 390.

'The Woodpecker', woven by William Morris, who had a great influence on nineteenth-century craftsmanship.

embroideries. Also some typical Morris furniture — rush-seated 'Sussex'-type settles and chairs of various designs, his reclining-back chair and later examples of cabinet-made furniture.

Some other interesting EXLEY titles now available

**See Britain at Work,
£4.95**
This guidebook details
hundreds of glassworks,
craft workshops,
potteries, factories etc.
open to the public and
to schools. An
invaluable family
reference book.

Shopping by Post, £5.50
Hundreds of firms
which will supply
goods by post. 'An
excellent book' (Marge
Proops).'Extraordinarily
comprehensive' (Sheila
Black). Invaluable for
those who live far from
good shops.

**Give Happiness a
Chance, £2.50**
Phil Bosmans'
thoughtful and poetic
book which has swept
Europe, with sales
approaching a million.
A memorable and
thoughtful gift.

Dear World, £6.95
'How I would put the
world right, by children
of 50 nations'. An
unusual and beautifully
illustrated book, in
colour.

**What is a husband?
£2.50**
7,500 real wives
answered that question
and the best quotes are
here. Pithy, beautiful,
rude, hilarious, sad,
romantic. Buy a copy
for your anniversary!

Old is great: £2.25
A book that pokes fun at
youth and revels in the
first grey hairs of middle-
age. 'An irreverent
sometimes bawdy, loo-
side book for anyone
over 30. Furiously
funny', says the Good
Book Guide.

**Grandmas & Grandpas,
£2.25**
'A Grandma is old on
the outside and young
on the inside.' This
charming little book
with all the entries
written by
grandchildren solves
many a present
problem.

To Dad, £2.25
'Fathers are always
right, and even if they're
not right, they're never
actually wrong.' Dads
will love this book. Also
in the series: *To Mum,
Happy Families, CATS
(and other crazy
cuddlies), DOGS (and
other funny furries).*

**All these books are obtainable through your local bookshop, or by
post from Exley Publications, 63 Kingsfield Road, Watford, Herts,
WD1 4PP. Please add 10p in the £ as a contribution to postage.**